Getting the Buggers to do their Homework

(2nd edition)

Other titles available in this series

Getting the Buggers Fit – Lorraine Cale and Joanne Harris
Getting the Buggers in Tune – Ian McCormack and Jeanette Healey
Getting the Buggers into Drama – Sue Cowley
Getting the Buggers into Languages 2nd Edition – Amanda Barton
Getting the Buggers into Science – Christine Farmery
Getting the Buggers Motivated in FE – Susan Wallace
Getting the Buggers to Add Up 2nd Edition – Mike Ollerton
Getting the Buggers to Behave 3rd Edition – Sue Cowley
Getting the Buggers to Draw - Barbara Ward
Getting the Buggers to Learn – Duncan Grey
Getting the Buggers to Learn in FE – Angela Steward
Getting the Buggers to Read 2nd Edition – Claire Senior
Getting the Buggers to Think 2nd Edition – Sue Cowley
Getting the Buggers to Turn Up – Ian McCormack
Getting the Buggers to Write – Sue Cowley
Letting the Buggers Be Creative – Sue Cowley

Also available from Continuum

Homework – Victoria Kidwell

Getting the Buggers to do their Homework

(2nd edition)

JULIAN STERN

continuum

Continuum International Publishing Group
The Tower Building, 11 York Road, London SE1 7NX
80 Maiden Lane, Suite 704, New York, NY 10038

www.continuumbooks.com

British Library Cataloguing-in-Publication Data
A catalogue record for this book is available from the British Library.

ISBN: 9-780-8264-9980-6 (paperback)

Library of Congress Cataloging-in-Publication Data
Stern, Julian.
   Getting the buggers to do their homework / Julian Stern. -- 2nd ed.
      p. cm.
   Includes bibliographical references and index.
   ISBN 978-0-8264-9980-6 (pb)
   1. Homework. I. Title.
   LB1048.S828 2009
   371.3'0821--dc22

                                                              2008039195

Typeset by Kenneth Burnley, Wirral, Cheshire
Printed and bound in Great Britain by MPG Books, Cornwall

Contents

Acknowledgements

The pleasure of writing a second edition, is the opportunity to revisit old ideas and discuss them with new colleagues. Thanks to Continuum, then, for inviting me to write this book.

For detailed comments and corrections for the first edition, and for improvements and additions to this second edition, I would like to thank Mike Bottery, John Buttrick of the Children's University Hull, Richard Clarke, Richard English, Karen Foster, Bethany James, Sarah James, Alex Montgomery, Peter Oates for Continuum Books, Anne Owen-Walker, Tina Page and her masters students, Sally Pryderi, Pam Rauchwerger, Marie Stern, Wendy Thompson (and Alex, Natasha and Dylan), Eamonn Whelan and Adrian Worsfold.

For their support and interest over 17 years of work on homework, I would like to thank colleagues, students, and pupils associated with South Camden Community School, the Prince's Trust, Östra Reals Gymnasium in Stockholm, the Open University, London University's Institute of Education, the University of Hull, and schools and education officials in the London Boroughs of Newham and Lambeth.

I am enormously grateful to David Fulton Publishers, who kindly gave their permission for the use of materials previously published by them in my book *Homework and Study Support* (Stern 1997a). I would also like to acknowledge the work of John MacBeath, which has done more than anything else to make this book possible, by treating homework seriously enough to be worth studying and worth providing professional guidance.

Preface

This is a book for teachers. It is not a book for teachers ambitious to know all the latest buzz words or theories, or ambitious to complete scholarly dissertations. It is not even a book intended to satisfy those ambitious for career progression and fame and fortune. This is a book for teachers who are ambitious for their pupils' learning, ambitious to make teaching and learning more valuable, interesting and effective, ambitious to help pupils grow and flourish. In this second edition, the book responds to

◆ comments of teachers from around the country;

◆ a number of new homework 'prophets of doom' such as Kohn (2006) and Bennett and Kalish (2006);

◆ several new government policies, such as the *Children's Plan*, that help support, and are supported by, homework.

As well as updating and adding to all the material, there is also much clearer guidance on homework in each subject. There are now over 200 individual homework tasks, across the whole curriculum.

Although this is a book for teachers, not parents, teaching assistants or pupils, it has been written so that readers who are not teachers may better understand what teachers can be doing about homework. Secrets are damaging in most areas of life. They are especially damaging when it comes to homework, as homework crosses many professional and personal boundaries. This book is therefore an open letter to teachers, to be read by anyone interested in the topic: anyone who loves or hates homework. The latter is well illustrated by a colleague of mine, who quizzed me about the title of the book, upset, they said, about the use of the rude word. I started justifying the use of the word 'bugger', but was interrupted. It was not *that* rude word. They were objecting to the use of the word 'homework'.

However much of a rude word homework is in your school (and all the evidence suggests that in most schools, homework is at best inconsistent), this book is intended to make it better. And making homework better will make classwork and home life better. Okay, it will not cure poverty or major illness . . . actually, now I come to think of it, perhaps it will overcome some of the disadvantages of poverty, and perhaps it will help inspire the doctors of the future. Anyway, eight decades of research papers on homework have demonstrated that not a lot has changed, so even a modest 'improving' ambition is well worth having.

As it says in the introduction (and in the introduction of every good book on homework), homework can be what learning is at its best: grabbing hold of the world and making it make sense for you. Now, get grabby.

Introduction:
hate homework, love homework

Why schools?

Some pupils ask why they have to do homework. They have the
wrong question. The peculiar thing is schoolwork, not homework. To
learn, people do not always need teachers, certainly not in the sense
we now think of teachers. Every language, apparently, has a word for
'learning'. Not every language has a word for 'teaching'. Through
most of history, people learned from their families, amateurs as
teachers, and from their peers and their colleagues.

How long have professional teachers been around? The age of
universal schooling, provided by professional teachers, has lasted no
more than a century in this country, less elsewhere. The age when
everyone expects a decade or more of schooling, alongside a lifetime
of learning, is a bit of an historical oddity.

Homework, or at least work outside the influence of a professional teacher, is therefore ancient and venerable. For thousands of
years, homework has been what everyone did: schoolwork has been
left to a tiny proportion of the population, and of those who did go
to school, this took up only a small proportion of their childhood.
15,000 hours of typical schooling is a small part of the 140,000 hours
of the first 16 years of life.

Learning out of school, at home, is therefore an everyday activity,
and this needs to be stressed to everyone, young and old, learner and
teacher. Homework has been around longer than classwork. That is
the point recently made in the *Children's Plan*, that 'government does
not bring up children – parents do – so government needs to do more
to back parents and families' (DCSF 2007: 5). But what have been
around even longer than homework, are love and hate.

Love and hate are closer than we may think. The people we love
are often the same as the people we hate, perhaps at different times.
We rarely love or hate people distant from us. It is those close to us,
often in our own families, whom we love or hate. The same goes for

homework: hated and loved, always close to us. If we are going to get pupils to do homework, the first lessons are therefore in hatred and love.

1. Why we hate homework: issues in time management, mistrust, administration and punishment

Homework is often hated. Indeed, one survey suggested that 50 per cent of children enjoyed school, but only 2 per cent enjoyed homework. A recent survey said that 'an overwhelming number of teachers say their pupils get upset or stressed with homework' (Milne 2008b). Homework can be seen as an unpleasant chore, a test only of the power of schools over pupils, rightly hated. Teachers are no greater fans than pupils; parents write to me of the traumas of their children's homework, and blame me (as a 'homework expert') for all the family rows on the topic.

There are at least four kinds of reason for everyone, teachers, pupils, families, hating homework. Homework takes time, and takes all the 'nicest' times, when you want to be watching television or playing computer games or sleeping. Homework creates mistrust amongst teachers, pupils and their families. Homework is an administrative nightmare of bits of paper and instructions and lists and mark books and deadlines. And homework is associated with the giving and receiving of punishments.

Here is my 'hate list' top 20, five reasons each for time, mistrust, administration and punishment. They are all coded, from **H1** to **H20**: it is useful if they could be ranked according to how much you agree with the reasons. Then, ask your colleagues and pupils how they would rank them.

Time-hates

H1 **Homework takes up a lot of time** of teachers, pupils and families. However, homework does not seem to have much effect on pupils' education. There is little solid research evidence of any impact of homework on pupil exam results, for example, and teachers will often admit that if a pupil does no homework, they can still succeed on their courses.

H2 **Homework takes time away from 'nice' things**: times that would otherwise be spent doing enjoyable things, entertaining things, even educational things like hobbies or clubs. Families may come back early from holidays, so that pupils can complete their homework tasks, or may prevent their children from going to dance classes or sports clubs because it will interfere with homework, or because, in combination, they would both interfere with sleep.

H3 **Homework time drags.** An hour spent doing homework often feels more like three hours doing something else, something more interesting, perhaps. Clocks and timetables make time seem very smooth and regular, but everyone knows that time shrinks or expands depending on the circumstances. Time flies, or drags. When doing homework, it most usually drags.

H4 **Homework takes preparation time and energy.** At least half the time spent on homework involves setting it up, clearing tables, sorting out the computer, getting rid of the brothers or sisters or cats or dogs. This takes time, and it also takes considerable energy and, in many homes, quite a bit of courage: it is not just dogs that bite.

H5 **Homework involves spending time worrying.** As well as the time spent doing homework, having homework also involves many hours spent worrying about it. The worry hours may be spent staring at the work, or at least staring past the work in order to see the television. As one correspondent said, 'If the homework was easy it was boring and if it was challenging you were scared that you were not doing the right thing'. Or as Russell Hoban says, homework 'sits on top of Sunday, squashing Sunday flat'.

Mistrust-hates

H6 **Homework breaks down classroom and home rule systems.** Teachers and pupils understand each other, in the sense that they know what the rules of the classroom are, even if they do not always follow them. Parents and children understand each other, in the sense that they know what the rules of the home are, even if they do not always follow them. Homework breaks down both sets of understanding, because it overlaps two systems of rules: it bridges the 'island' of school and the 'mainland' of home. It can therefore spoil both sets of relationships, and create mistrust between all three groups.

H7 **Teachers introduce homework with expressions of mistrust.** Teachers often express their mistrust of pupils when giving out homework, as homework is seen as trying to get pupils to do something when the teacher is not there to check. It is not a good idea for a teacher to leave a class alone, so imagine leaving pupils alone to do their homework. Teachers therefore introduce homework with expressions of mistrust, or fears that pupils will cheat by copying things from the computer or from each other. Many teachers see homework as a way of checking that the pupils have been concentrating in class, which can add to the sense of mistrust.

H8 **Teachers express mistrust when taking in homework.** For much the same reason, teachers often express their mistrust of pupils when taking in homework. There are many adults who will say how traumatized they were when they put a huge amount of effort into a piece of homework, only for the teacher to say 'You must have got someone else to do it, it is much too good for you'. (Not so many are prepared to admit the occasions when they did indeed cheat, of course.)

H9 **Parents show mistrust through homework.** Parents often show their mistrust of their children through homework: they may not believe children are really doing their homework, when in another room, and they may not believe children do not have any homework, even if none has been set.

H10 **Pupils do not trust teachers to be setting homework for educational reasons**: they often think, quite rightly, that teachers simply feel obliged to set homework. They are also often aware that homework tasks are impossible: sometimes impossible for anyone, often impossible for the pupil in their own circumstances. This leads to a bigger loss of trust, as pupils may question the educational purpose of all the work of their teachers, and may end up in trouble for what is, in practice, the teacher's fault.

Administrative-hates

H11 **Homework is hard to organize.** Homework not only takes twice as long as it should, because the pupil has to clear away the dishes or chase out the siblings, it is also hard to organize. There are materials that you take to school, and that, if you forget, can be borrowed or replaced. Homework is harder to organize for, and the pens, or colours, or glue, or paper, or books, or instructions are – if absent – much harder to compensate for or replace, as few have the materials at home that would be available at school.

H12 It is difficult getting the homework back to school. Even if the work is completed, despite the risks of not having the right materials to hand, and is completed on the right day, there is the problem of getting the homework back to school. Just because 99 in every 100 times pupils say 'I did my homework but I forgot to bring it in' they are fibbing, there is still that 1 per cent of cases when it is true. Pupils will be embarrassed when this happens, and pupils who are good liars will feign this embarrassment, which will make the 'real' embarrassment even more embarrassing.

H13 Homework is often set in a hurry, at the end of the lesson. For teachers, setting homework is often seen as a much greater challenge than setting classwork. It is often the last thing to be thought of, the last thing to be organized and resourced, and is set at the worst possible moment: the very end of the lesson. Experienced teachers will have 'fall-back' homework, for when they have not planned any in advance. The two most popular spontaneous tasks are 'Finish off' and (when no test has as yet been prepared) 'Revise for a test'. But the hatred is still there, exacerbated by the end-of-lessonness it exhibits: 94 per cent of homework tasks, in one study, were set at the end of the lesson, half of them after the bell had rung, and in 9 per cent of cases *during the ringing of the bell.*

H14 Checking on and marking homework make teachers hate it even more. Teachers know whether a pupil is working in class, and can easily re-engage the pupil if off-task. Homework needs checking, and a teacher with 500 homework tasks to be handed in every week (a common experience for teachers, such as RE or music teachers, with a large number of classes seen once a week), can feel the checking alone, never mind the marking, is a full-time job. Marking can be even more hateful, especially if the task to be marked is very routine. Homework for pupils creates homework for teachers.

H15 Teachers are inspected and held accountable for implementing homework. Schools are all supposed to have homework policies and procedures, with timetables usually arranged so that one year group will expect to have 20 minutes of homework set every Tuesday, and another will have 40 minutes every Friday. Teachers are held accountable for implementing the policy, which means inspection and checking and complaints if it all goes wrong: complaints from pupils, parents, school managers and anyone else with an interest in annoying teachers.

Punishment-hates

H16 **Teachers associate homework with punishment.** Pupils who miss school will, on their return, be welcomed back and asked how they are and helped to catch up; pupils who miss a lot of school may be referred to social workers and educational psychologists. Pupils who miss homework will be given a detention; pupils who miss a lot of homework will either be given a lot of detentions or, worse, have the absence of homework attributed to bad parenting.

H17 **Parents associate homework with punishment** or at least see it as an unpleasant activity. Grumpy parents force their children to complete homework, and use homework as a lever: 'You are not going out until you've done your homework'.

H18 **Homework is associated with punishment by otherwise amenable pupils.** Pupils who are generally well behaved in school will usually have had the experience of being punished for not handing in homework. Many will also have had the experience of 'getting away' with not getting punished despite not handing in homework. In these ways, homework is associated with punishment and with poor enforcement of punishments.

H19 **Pupils may prefer the punishment to the homework:** a lunchtime or after-school detention (if that is the punishment) is seen as rather more pleasant than an evening worrying over homework. In that sense homework, ironically, is often worse than punishment.

H20 **Teachers may prefer the abolition of homework to a pay rise.** When teachers are asked whether they would prefer a pay rise or the abolition of homework, many would opt for the latter, as it would, they say, make their lives much more pleasant. No worrying about setting homework, no hassles with checking and marking homework, and no unpleasant confrontations with otherwise amenable pupils who have not completed their homework.

There is nothing much wrong with hatred, unless you let it eat you up inside, and do nothing about it. A recent advert said 'Hate something: change something'. Not a bad principle. The rest of this book addresses the 'change' issues, with Chapter 1 focusing on overcoming some of the time problems, Chapters 2 and 3 building up greater trust, Chapters 4 and 5 looking at administration and organization, and every chapter helping us avoid punishment (though there are also some sneaky ideas on punishments in Chapter 5). All the hate-codes (from **H1** to **H20**) are mentioned whenever an idea is described that helps change or avoid them: do check them, to see if you agree. Meanwhile, consider love.

2. Why we love homework: issues in applied learning, individual interests and inclusion

Homework can be what learning is at its best: grabbing hold of the world and making it make sense for you. How many adults still have, hidden away, some piece of work done years ago at school, a project on the Incas, or a story for the school magazine? Of all the 'kept' pieces of work, most were completed largely or entirely at home. In college and university education, the most remembered products are the dissertations done in the library and in college rooms, not the notes taken in lectures, seminars and tutorials.

Are you more fluent in the language you learnt in the classroom, or the language you learnt at home, aged nothing, or on holiday? There is a good basis for promoting homework, then, as the most exciting, memorable, side of education. It is what we love most about our school days. It is the way in which we actively demonstrate what we know, rather than passively responding, in class, to a teacher's request for one-word answers.

Pupils who can complete homework are learning independently, and are applying classwork beyond the classroom. Often enough, homework is a chance to do something distinctive and original, a chance to show off what you know about a topic that is a real interest of yours. Some children do not get much of a chance to talk and work creatively with friends and family: homework can encourage such work. More than that, it can show pupils that the school 'recognizes' their homes and communities, and can show family members that the school has, or should have, relevance to their lives.

Here is my 'love list': 20 reasons to love homework, addressing issues in applied learning, individual interests and inclusion. As with the hate list, they are coded (from **L1** to **L20**): rank them according to how much you agree with the reasons. Then, ask your colleagues and pupils how they would rank them.

Applied-loves

L1 **Homework can carry fascination into the life-long hobby or career.** Go on, admit it. There was something at school that was interesting. It may not be very fashionable to say that learning is interesting, but almost everyone can describe something truly fascinating from their school days. The sign of fascination is that it goes beyond the lessons themselves. A fascination with history lessons turns into following television or web-based history or visiting ancient monuments, a fascination with science turns into a career in the chemical industry. When such fascinations are investigated, the 'carrier' of the fascination is often homework.

A teacher lets someone borrow a book on a topic, another says that pupils should really watch a programme that evening, another makes pupils see the heart as a wonderful machine by getting them to take their pulse throughout the day. The Thursday evening homework can become the life-long hobby or career.

L2 **Homework generates conversation, not junk chat.** People learn in conversation, not just by listening to teachers. For some, dialogue is the essence of what makes us human. Less philosophically, conversation allows us to test out ideas and ways of living. This can be seen in the consequences of having difficulty engaging in conversation. People on the autistic spectrum, identified in part by such difficulty, may find it hard making connections between different aspects of what has been learned, and may be regarded by others as unusual or eccentric.

It is homework that provides the widest range of opportunities for conversation. It may be conversation between pupils (rehearsing a presentation), or between pupils and their families (asking for support or interviewing them for a geography project). Effective homework provides fuel for conversations. Just as school dinners should provide nourishment for the body, whatever nourishment and junk food is available beyond the school, homework should provide nourishment for conversations, whatever the competition is from junk chat.

L3 **Argument is a reason to love homework, creating the next generation.** Conversation can lead to argument, and argument is a reason to love homework. Teachers of sociology will have tales of arguments in pupils' homes about gender roles, teachers of science and geography will tell of arguments about recycling, teachers of religion know of arguments about what Muslims believe. Arguments can be unpleasant and destructive. They can also be positive, a way of growing up and understanding the differences in the world.

Parents often talk with a wry smile about how their children have argued them into a different way of life, a fitness regime or changed attitudes to racism. Schools are not there to change families, of course: they have enough to do already. Yet homework can be the basis for creating the next generation, with its own distinctive way of looking at the world, its own arguments.

L4 **Homework generates the most memorable work.** The most memorable pieces of work are often those largely completed for homework, and there are good psychological reasons for this, related to memory and the contexts of learning. What it boils down to is the tendency of classes to involve more dependence on the teacher, and homework tasks (when they work) to involve more independence. Memory is about possession, and independent learning allows us to possess what is learned.

L5 **Homework is memorable for other family members**, as well as for pupils. Most homes have a fridge gallery or its equivalent: the young child's paintings of houses, trees, family members and big yellow suns. There is an equivalent for older pupils, the products of lessons (including art work, still), and the by-products of lessons such as certificates and trophies. As the children get older, the products of their education are often most memorable because they have involved the home and family and friends.

No more than a grunt, or an embarrassing moment at a parents' evening, greets family enquiries into classwork, but pride and even the occasional 'Wow' can greet the realization of the talents of a secondary pupil successfully completing a piece of engaging homework.

L6 **Teachers have a joy in the best homework.** Their praise of excellent homework has an additional edge to it, and is received by pupils with more pleasure. There is often an unstated 'You didn't really have to do it to this quality, but I am really proud of you that you did', matched by 'I don't mind doing what I regard as extra work if it pleases the teacher'. Whether homework really is 'additional', the giving and receiving of praise makes the best homework well loved. Sometimes, others get caught in the wash of praise, when parents or siblings are directly or indirectly complimented for their contribution to the homework.

L7 **Homework is loved as the opportunity to get lost in work**, as it allows pupils to work uninterrupted for an extended period of time. No interruptions from other pupils or from teachers. Extended work allows for the application of classroom learning, it allows pupils to work through a problem rather than just survive until the end of the lesson or the end of the task. Homework can be loved as the opportunity to get lost in work.

Being lost in work may involve being absorbed by an activity, making something, or absorbed by a process, searching for ideas or information. It may involve experiencing what Csikszentmihalyi (2002) calls 'flow'.

L8 **For teachers, homework means their teaching works beyond them.** Teachers also want pupils to get lost: get lost in their work, of course. It is what teachers love most, because it means that their teaching works beyond them. Teaching creates a legacy when it happens if the teacher is not there. Or as Einstein apparently said, 'Education is what remains after one has forgotten what one has learned in school'.

L9 **Teachers admit the world beyond the school, through homework.** Victorian schools were often built with windows high on the walls, so that the pupils would not be distracted by 'the outside world' whilst studying. Homework can be loved as an admission of the breaching of that isolation. Even the excuses, the dogs eating the homework, the siblings or parents rowing, the unexpected visitor from India, admit to this connection. Successful, completed, homework admits to it even more. Computers have helped people see the ways of overcoming barriers of space (through world-wide connectivity) and time (through any-time access and asynchronous chat), but homework was always a little sign of this breach.

L10 **Homework exploits all the resources of the school.** Homework is not always completed at home. Venues include libraries, buses, cars and parks. The most popular non-home venue, though, is the school. For many pupils, the school is the best place to complete homework, away from the distractions of home and close to much needed human and material resources. It is a particularly good venue for group work. Pupils can be found rehearsing a role-play, organizing a group project such as a newspaper, discussing positions in a debate, combining web searches on the school computers.

School libraries and computer suites, lunch halls, social areas, playgrounds, corridors and empty classrooms: all can come alive with clusters of pupils completing homework. Pupils may love school-based homework because it gives them a purpose to be in school for longer than lesson-time alone, and a good reason to work with other pupils. Teachers may love school-based homework because it exploits all the resources of the school, and avoids teachers needing to supervise what would otherwise be a mixture of play and loneliness.

Individual-loves

L11 Homework promotes individual pride and success. It is not just that homework is, in various senses, 'applied' classwork that is important. Homework can and should involve doing something that interests each individual pupil. There are good reasons for classwork having a common core; there are even better reasons for homework stressing the individual interests of pupils. Teachers know that 30 pupils completing the same routine task will learn less than 30 pupils completing distinct individual tasks.

A teacher who asks every pupil to create an Advent Calendar for homework, as part of learning about Christmas, may get some excellent work from several pupils. A teacher who asks each pupil to create an exciting single day, from one to 24, for a giant whole-class advent calendar, will be likely to get worthwhile work from every pupil, and excellent work from most. Homework is lovable for its ability to promote individual pride and success.

L12 In promoting homework, teachers are indispensably dispensable. All teachers would like to think they are irreplaceable, but pupils need time to get away from teachers. This growing independence is healthy, and the older pupils get, the more they need to be able to work independently. Homework can get the teacher off your back.

It can be a relief to work uninterrupted, perhaps on your own computer or in your own room. Even if it is no relief, it is necessary, for real independent learning to take place. Homework should be loved for this reason, and if it is, then the homework will be successful, and the teacher will have achieved quite something. Teachers are irreplaceable, after all.

L13 Homework cures boredom. Homework is hated for being boring; it is loved for curing boredom. Boredom is associated with passive, repetitious and meaningless tasks; its cure is therefore engagement and individuality and purpose. If adolescent pupils suffer from boredom, then homework is a solution. Not many pupils will admit that homework cures boredom, yet it often does.

Teachers, no less than pupils, may find searching for and editing materials from the internet an enthralling task during which the hours fly by; likewise, reading a book, sketching a relative, thinking of 50 questions to suit a single answer. A trip to an art gallery can take hours, with a simple task added of choosing the three paintings that you would take to a desert island, and giving good reasons for each choice. (One eccentric pupil at the National Gallery chose one of Monet's pictures of waterlillies, not for its artistic merit, but the large quantity of wood it would supply for a raft to escape the island.)

L14 Homework celebrates pupils' distinctive and individual lives. Pupils lead many lives outside school. If homework understands that, the distinctive and individual lives led by pupils can be celebrated in the homework itself. This is rarely achieved in the rather tired 'What I did in my holiday' homework: tired and open to unhealthy competition between pupils, keen to demonstrate the exoticism of their holiday, or embarrassed by its absence. It can, however, be achieved by homework tasks that capture the streets and people and cultures and objects in the worlds of pupils. The capture may be geographical, for geographers; artistic, linguistic, historic, religious, musical, scientific or physical, for teachers of those subjects.

L15 Homework cures deadlinitis. Homework can be the way to cure the harm caused by deadlines. Deadlines are unpleasant creatures. They hang around in the shadows, occasionally calling out to pupils, hoping not to hear them. Being left alone in the shadows, they get hungrier and hungrier, until, eventually, they pounce, giving pupils cold sweats and sleepless nights. Soon after this, the deadlines die peacefully, leaving pupils feeling bloodless and drained. Yet deadlines are perfectly fair. If you feed them steadily through the year, they will not ask for any more food than if the feeding is left to the last minute.

Homework is often the source of unpleasant deadlines. Douglas Adams, author of *The Hitchhiker's Guide to the Galaxy* and notorious for missing deadlines, apparently wanted his gravestone to read 'He finally met his deadline'. Yet if a pupil has the right approach to deadlines, then the individual control over work, the ability to plan a piece of work over time, the ability to take responsibility for what might be a project extended over several weeks, will be one of the best achievements of a pupil's life at or, rather, outside school. Love homework for its insistence on overcoming deadlinitis.

Inclusive-loves

L16 Homework enriches the curriculum by including pupils as they are. The curriculum has its own intrinsic and extrinsic worth, listed in the introductions to most curriculum documents. Brought to the curriculum is a set of ideas and wisdom from many adults. Homework, more than classwork, can enrich the curriculum by bringing in to the curriculum more ideas and more wisdom from both pupils and other adults in and beyond their families. If schools are truly inclusive, recognizing and giving meaning to the lives of all their pupils, homework is the way of achieving this. Homework includes pupils as they are and as they live, and the curriculum is all the richer for that.

L17 Homework captures and exploits resources from beyond the school. Schools are under-resourced. All will fight for better resources in schools. Homework, meanwhile, can capture and exploit the cornucopia of resources beyond the school. More or less formal resource banks exist outside the school: libraries, museums, televisions, computers, homes, shops, galleries, parks, cafés, gardens and travel agents. It is homework if pupils make use of these resources and it is an improvement to education if the resources available to pupils are expanded to include those beyond the school.

L18 Homework exploits people (in and outside school) as resources. It should hardly need saying that people are the most valuable resources of all. Homework can exploit people as resources. People outside of school, or people inside school but outside lessons (pupils, the most useful supporters of homework and teachers, along with lunch staff and premises staff and office staff), friends or relatives: homework is the way all these people can contribute to and improve the curriculum, with pupils as the carriers of their knowledge and understanding. This is a good reason for loving homework.

L19 Homework inspires encouragement from beyond school. Pupils should gain support and encouragement from teachers in school. (There is some evidence that this is not recognized by all pupils: more of that later, in the section on 'help me' homework.) Encouragement from outside the school complements encouragement from within. Homework should be of a nature to inspire such encouragement, but the encouragement can be built in to the homework itself. Work with adults on what has changed over time, or work with adults to make a meal, can benefit all concerned. Interviews on beliefs, giving and receiving advice on design around the home, or working out how to improve the environment, can be positively therapeutic.

L20 Homework creates positive connections across the school. There are many opportunities for group work homework, as described above in 'applied-loves'. This kind of work is also to be loved because it furthers the inclusiveness of the school. Homework can encourage pupils to work with people they might not otherwise have worked with: younger pupils, older pupils, adults other than teachers, pupils with different beliefs and ways of living. The sensitive bringing together of people from across the school, through homework, will make the school a better place for all.

A study of troubled teenagers tried to find out why some were involved in attacking and robbing the elderly, whilst others, equally troubled and equally involved in crime, avoided harming the elderly: the latter group had grandparents who were regularly visited. As simple as that. Connection meant understanding meant an unwillingness to attack. Within the school, homework can create such positive connections.

These reasons to love homework are inevitably used throughout the book, with the 'applied-loves' especially covered in Chapters 2 and 5, the 'individual-loves' in Chapters 1, 2 and 4, and the 'inclusive-loves' in Chapters 3 and 4. Every time a love issue is addressed in the rest of the book, there is a note '(L15)' indicating which of the love-codes is particularly addressed. In the index, there is also a guide to where each of the love-codes and hate-codes is addressed. It is also worth considering, here, how all of this fits into a pattern: an explanation of what kinds of homework exist. Homework is, after all, as homework does.

3. Homework is as homework does

In conclusion to this love–hate relationship with homework, it can be repeated that there is not much research on whether or how much homework helps attainment in school, though it seems most useful for lower-ability pupils, and may be associated with positive attitudes to school and with excellent rather than just satisfactory Ofsted reports. (For more evidence, see Chapter 5.) Yet, having looked at reasons to love and hate homework, it is clear how to get the buggers to do their homework: set them homework that is useful (that expands learning time), relevant (that is applicable to pupils' lives), and makes use of the fact that it is homework (that captures the world beyond the school).

That is the short answer to the question of homework. The long answer takes up the rest of the book, which is built on the same three-stage model of homework: expansion, application and capture.

◆ *First*, we could use homework to 'expand' the 15,000 hours of schooling currently endured by children. This is based on the idea that there are not enough hours in the school day to complete all the learning needed. The 'expansion' model of homework includes 'finishing off' and related 'Just do a bit more' homework tasks, the worst kinds of homework, unnecessarily stressful and inefficient. Yet at its best it is a worthwhile addition to school. The best side of expansion homework is described in Chapter 1.

Favourite *expansion* homework tasks include:

• Working out 25 questions whose answer is 100 (p. 24).
• Letters between an agony aunt and an historical or literary figure (pp. 32–3).
• Completing the missing half of a torn page (p. 35).

◆ *Second*, homework could be used in such a way that the 15,000 hours of schooling could be 'applied' to the rest of the child's world. This model implies that school subjects need to be relevant, and school learning consists of a set of 'apprenticeships' in the world, with the pupils understanding the value of school learning and the value of their world, through homework. Different aspects of such application homework are described in Chapter 2.

Favourite *application* homework tasks include:

- Imagine you are members of the 'religion police' (p. 44).
- Analysing biases in particular television programmes (pp. 52–3).
- Reviewing the school prospectus or website (p. 57).

◆ *Third*, homework could be used to ensure that the remaining 125,000 hours of childhood be made use of in school: homework 'captures' the child's world for the schoolwork. This may be based on the idea of 'exploiting' homes, a sort of recycling of home 'stuff' in school. Homework can 'catch people out' learning when they least expect it: in their homes.

This idea is an old idea that has been revived in various recent government initiatives. The *Every Child Matters* policy says that all children's services should help promote learning, and that schooling should promote all aspects of children's development – their health, safety, enjoyment of life, making a positive contribution and economic well-being. That work will need all children's services to work together, and all to work with children and their families and carers. 'Parent partnerships' and the importance of families is stressed in the *Children's Plan*. Such policies are related to the growth of 'extended schools' (see Chapter 5), where schools are seen as more than places for lessons. Welcome back, homework.

Homework can also help pupils become more human. Pupils learn how to be human in school (that is what personal, social, cultural and spiritual development mean), and they do this by working within the school community. School communities are halfway houses, between families and broader social groups. Homework can therefore capture aspects of other communities, in order to help pupils and the staff within the school. Schooling helps to make, or make more possible, a community of communities in and beyond school. In these ways, homework creates more inclusive schooling. Chapter 3 covers various kinds of capture homework.

Favourite *capture* homework tasks include:

◆ Completing speech bubbles around Picasso's *Guernica* (p. 63).

◆ Keeping an 'ecology journal' for life outside school (pp. 70–1).

◆ Creating a study guide for next year's pupils (p. 82).

Getting the pupils to do their homework, therefore, means understanding what homework is for and how it works, and then getting the teachers, the professionals, to set the best kinds of homework. Admitting some of the disadvantages as well as advantages of homework is part of this process, and Chapter 4 investigates the abolition of homework and the rest of homework that dares not speak its name. Being resourceful, juggling the resources to be used for homework, and finding out more about how homework and learning work, is covered by Chapter 5.

Favourite *abolition* homework tasks include:

◆ Round-the-house revision (p. 89).

◆ Contributing to a subject-class blog (p. 93).

◆ Describing bridges seen whilst on holiday (p. 97).

And if anyone asks you, 'What, exactly, do you mean by homework?', MacBeath and Turner (1990) say that homework is learning 'that is relevant to teachers' curricular objectives . . . which takes place outwith formal classroom teaching . . . which is primarily the responsibility of the learner himself/herself'.

My definition of homework is therefore simple. Homework happens when pupils learn what the school wants them to learn, away from the classroom and away from teachers.

In the following chapters are over 200 different homework tasks, explained in ways that will allow teachers and pupils to create hundreds more tasks.

1 | Expansion homework: extending the school

Homework in this chapter

We need more school, don't we?

The world of the classroom is important, the lessons are important. If only we had a little more time. Most of my lessons were like the episode of *The Simpsons* set on the last day of term when the last bell goes. The pupils run out of the school. The history teacher who has been teaching the Second World War shouts 'Wait: you don't know how it finishes'. The pupils stop in their tracks; the teacher announces 'We won!' Everyone runs off for their holidays.

That last 'We won!' was a tiny expansion of the time spent on classwork. Of course, the most exciting and enthralling classwork expands itself: we get to the end of a lesson and everyone wants to keep going. Goodness knows, that is not what happens at the end of every lesson, but it is still a healthy aspiration. If one lesson a year for each group is so engrossing that the pupils do not want the lesson to end, then we are doing something right.

Meanwhile, back on planet earth, there are several ways of setting homework that can expand the 15,000 hours of time available in lessons. If the homework is organized well, this expansion of time will help solve some time management problems within lessons whilst avoiding some of the time management problems described in the litany of hatred in the introduction. The victory over time, if achieved, is well worthwhile, as 'over the five years of secondary education, appropriate homework can add the equivalent of at least one additional year of full-time education' (Hargreaves 1984).

Doing homework or not doing homework: the equivalent of a full year's worth of lessons. Keep saying that to yourself, as readers of Hargreaves' report have been doing for over 20 years, especially when tempted to ignore homework for some pupils or some classes. If we think education is worthwhile, if we believe in equal opportunities, if we believe in giving all pupils a good education, what can we do to make sure that no pupils lose the 'homework year'?

The section on 'Keep going' homework is about the basic expansion of lesson time, trying to avoid the most often set, and one of the most hated, of homework tasks: 'Finish off'. New parents usually promise to themselves never to use the phrases that they hated their parents for saying, such as 'What time do you call this?', 'You're not going out dressed like *that*!', and 'Because I say so'. Teachers should promise themselves not to utter certain phrases, amongst which are 'Colour this in', 'Education is wasted on you', 'Why aren't you more like your brother/sister' (or 'You are turning into your brother/sister'), 'Shut up', 'Don't be so stupid', any phrase using the word 'but' (as in the phrase 'Very good work, but why couldn't you . . .'), and especially 'Finish this off for homework'.

New parents soon find themselves unavoidably drawn to the occasional use of the forbidden phrases (as their parents had been, before them), and teachers may also occasionally find the temptation too great. But, to use a term to be avoided, teachers should feel guilty, and renew their promise to avoid the phrases. 'Finish off' homework tasks are unfair and unreasonable. They are unfair because they penalize slower workers and reward quicker workers, which usually (though by no means always) penalizes the lower-achieving pupils and rewards the higher-achieving pupils. They are unreasonable because the pupils (notably the slower-working pupils) are likely to need a teacher's support for classwork (otherwise, why was the task being completed in class time in the first place?), so finishing off outside class is likely to be the hardest task of all, yet having no professional support.

It is parents who usually end up supporting such work. Finishing off may therefore make the parents or other family members into substitute teachers, but substitute teachers without the pay or the qualifications that substitute teachers would normally have, working in conditions at home that are less appropriate than classroom conditions.

Finishing off is also usually very boring, and boring tasks are not the best to set for homework. Some teachers have been heard to say 'I will set this work for homework, because it is too boring for classwork'. If there has to be boring work, then it is usually better that it be completed in class, with a teacher to encourage the pupils through the long boring hours and able to say 'It may be boring, but it is worthwhile, because . . .'. Homework, in contrast, needs to be more interesting than classwork if the homework is a straightforward extension of classwork, because there are so many distractions, and so little specialist academic support, in homes. A father is quoted by MacBeath and Turner (1990), saying

> I am getting a mite scunnered wi' the words. I can see they have to do them but could they not make it a wee bit mair interesting wi' puzzles or crosswords. Dress it up, you know what I mean.

So here are various ideas for 'dressing up' the kinds of homework tasks that are, in essence, expanding the lesson-time. Some are ways of keeping the lesson going after the lesson has finished, others are ways of using homework to help the teacher (perhaps overcoming teachers' hatred of homework), and some are examples of ham-mocking: helping improve even the most boring tasks.

1. 'Keep going' homework

The UK government has said (in DfEE 1998b, DfES 2004) that pupils aged 11 to 13 should spend 45 to 90 minutes a day on homework, with 60–120 minutes a day for 13–14 year olds, and 90–150 minutes for 14–16 year olds. Even if only the smaller of the figures were achieved, this would be enough to add at least a year's worth of edu-cation for secondary pupils, or 20 per cent more time. When teachers are asked how much homework pupils complete, they guess lower figures than this. Pupils have different views again. What is clear is that very little is clear. The first suggestion is therefore that it is worthwhile teachers knowing how much time homework takes.

Pupils should be asked to write the number of minutes spent on the homework task in *all subjects* (either on the task itself or in the homework diary if that is well used). It is surprising how good this is for honesty. Pupils are reluctant to exaggerate the number of minutes spent on a piece of work, as it might give the impression that they are less able than they would like to be; pupils are reluctant to under-state the number of minutes spent on a piece of work, as it might lead to an inflation in future homework tasks. So pupils are, generally, honest.

That means teachers will know how much extra time is added by homework. Is this above or below the rough average of 20 per cent of lesson time? If it is radically below or above that percentage, then there are opportunities for change. Remember that the time pupils spend *learning* is more important than the time spent by teachers *teaching*.

It is worth noting that pupils may be more honest than parents. A recent survey reported in the *Times Educational Supplement* (*TES*) (Milne 2008a) was based on the views of 'more than 75,000 parents'. 'It shows that on average, pupils in the wealthier areas do 5.66 hours a week of homework, while those in poor areas do 4.35 hours'. In fact, it is just as likely to show the difference between the expectations and awareness of parents. In wealthier areas, children have more opportunities to hide away in a separate room, saying they are doing their homework whilst actually enjoying themselves.

This is the message of an American study of parents and teachers, which reported a problem with affluence. In affluent communities 'the houses are just much too big'. 'Everyone goes to his corner of the house, behind closed doors, and the parents do not see the action. I feel the same way about these big cars, these huge vans. The kids sit way in the back of the car and the parents have no idea what they are doing.' (Lawrence-Lightfoot 2003: 175.)

Pupils are therefore more likely to know and, if asked in the right way, be honest about the number of minutes they spend doing homework. Developing this bean-counting idea, try setting limits on homework. Teachers who think pupils hate doing homework may think it absurd to set an upper time limit on a homework task. However, by setting such a limit, there should be less stress for those pupils who try to do homework well, and there may well be an incentive for pupils to do 'extra' homework, so as to appear really 'clever' in apparently completing so much homework in such a short time. Teachers would be shocked if told that their lesson should last 'as long as it takes', or that some pupils should have more lessons than others, and that they may not feel the need to have any lessons one week, if the previous week's lessons were particularly good. Yet the same is all too often said of homework.

Flexibility may be a good thing and certainly sounds ideal for homework. However, a constant, vigorous, complaint from pupils is that it is unfair to be given homework in 'lumps', with none for several weeks then all subjects in one week. This often happens a couple of weeks into each term (week one: be kind; week two: set a big homework; week three: collect the homework), and two weeks before a holiday (better get a homework set before the last week of term, so it can be marked before the holiday). In practice, such homework is not genuinely flexible, just badly planned and lumpy.

A rigid homework timetable may be disliked by teachers, resenting interference, but it can benefit pupils. It will help pupils to organize their work if teachers set realistically time-limited homework tasks within an overall limit, i.e. minutes per week in every subject. It will engage pupils even more if they are involved in developing a pattern of homework timings, for example through a school council, a questionnaire, or representatives at department meetings.

Tasks that can be set, that are at the more effective end of the 'Keep going' scale, include the following:

◆ Special games or puzzles, started in class but to be finished outside class, work well as occasional homework tasks, and can pass the time wonderfully well. There are hard **maths** tasks, such as using exactly three 3s and mathematical symbols to generate every number from 0 to 10. Three 3s could be replaced by four 4s, too, and both could be replaced with the difficult but popular *Su Doku* puzzles. **(L1)**

- Try, in **English**, to find the longest words that can be played on a musical instrument (i.e. using the letters A to G), or that have all the letters in alphabetical order, or that have no letters appearing more than once, or that have horizontal symmetry when written in upper case letters, or that are anagrams of each other. The list goes on and on. **(H4)**
- Easier **maths** puzzles would be to ask pupils to think of 25 questions with answers of 100, or to think up a piece of writing with each word starting with the letters of the alphabet in order (for example 'A big cat drives elephants frantic'). **(H3)**
- Puzzle-type investigations of more immediate personal relevance, again needing to be started in class but able to be continued beyond, might include:

  analysing each pupil's 'ecological footprint' in **geography**, as at www.myfootprint.org/ or www.rprogress.org/ or with an 'ecoquiz' at www.reep.org.uk,

  calculating life expectancy for **PSHE**, using various health measures, as at www.livingto100.com/,

  estimating expected GCSE or A Level grades based on demographic statistics (on UpMyStreet at www.upyourstreet.co.uk/) or inspection information (from www.ofsted.gov.uk) or the detailed Yellis and related programmes from the University of Durham (www.yellisproject.org/ and www.alisproject.org/ and www.midyisproject.org/).

These activities can generate some powerful and creative arguments between pupils and even more within families. **(L3)**

♦ Developing extended writing for homework tasks is a worthwhile challenge in **English** and other subjects. Extended writing should be started in class, and can be continued after class: it is not helpful, at any level, restricting such writing to homework alone. Pupils often find extended writing tasks difficult, because of the difficulty of planning and structuring them, but if they are given no opportunity to practise, they will never develop the skills.

One technique is to start, in class, by giving pupils opening sentences for each paragraph of an essay, allowing them to use these sentences or their own. The class may even come to agreement on which sentences work best as starters. This has proved useful for those pupils who prefer very short, structured exercises. The work might be of a simple descriptive kind (for example writing-up field-work or an experiment), or of an imaginative kind (such as planning for floods or for a celebration of someone's birth). **(H13)**

♦ More practical skills can be developed in 'Keep going' homework. A group of pupils working on Native American history and culture in **history** might be asked to use the ideas learned in class to design a totem pole for homework, with the designs then being the basis for an extended holiday homework task asking the pupils to make their totem poles. 'Marking' such homework becomes a thoroughly positive and celebratory experience. **(H14)**

♦ Cross-curricular work, related to **citizenship**, such as writing as if a government minister, or as if a candidate for a job working for a pressure group, could inspire extended writing tasks. This could also inspire extended *speaking* tasks, if pupils were asked to plan a speech, to be given in class. Either way, the teacher will be affecting the pupils whilst the pupils are 'out of reach'. **(L8)**

♦ Teachers who find themselves at the end of a lesson, with no idea what to set for homework, are liable to say 'I think we'll have a test next lesson: the homework is to revise for the test'. This is not unreasonable, at least if the teacher is clear about what should be revised. In other words, the pupils can be 'kept going' on a topic, or on the development of a particular skill, simply by being told that these aspects of the topic or skill will be tested in the next lesson. Indeed, with a little more preparation, a test can be given out in class, with the homework task being to research the answers, and the test being set 'officially' in the next lesson.

A useful technique, whenever revision is set as homework, is to ask the pupils at the start of the next lesson whether they have done the homework: most, presumably, will say they have. Then, when the tests are marked and given back, the teacher can say 'Considering you all revised for the test, these marks are not as good as I had expected'. On such occasions, pupils have been known to insist on telling you that they did *not* do any homework: a rarity, this, and very helpful in creating a more trusting atmosphere. **(H8)**

◆ Research or other investigative tasks started in class are popular for teachers when setting homework. Such tasks, because they involve independent learning, have built-in motivation, and teachers can appreciate their own independence: they are helping create learners who do not always need teachers standing at their shoulders. (This form of homework appears in another form in Chapter 4, as 'abolition' homework.) **(L8)**

◆ Keeping going is itself often most difficult in the first few weeks of secondary school, when pupils are usually keenest and yet least skilled in juggling the various demands of separate subjects and separate teachers. (There is a similar, slightly smaller, crisis point at the start of GCSEs and at the start of AS levels.) Unco-ordinated homework in these weeks can cause long-term damage to relationships with pupils and with homes.

Pupils could be given a single booklet containing homework in every subject for two or three weeks, including which nights each homework task should be completed and handed in. A booklet like this could be planned and agreed by all staff, perhaps based around a theme like 'myself' or 'home and school'. On 'myself', here are some suggested activities:

English homework might include a language history,

maths might involve work on measurements,

science might involve work on pulses,

history on a personal time-line,

geography on places visited,

RE on personal symbols,

MFL on saying 'My name is . . .' in different languages,

art on self-portraiture,

music on personal musical tastes,

technology on favourite objects or foods,

PE on a health and fitness audit, and

ICT on a database collecting all this information.

A well-coordinated set of homework tasks in these first weeks can do a great deal to help teachers and parents or carers to work a 'pincer movement' on the children: working together to stress the importance of this new phase of the children's lives. **(H6)**

2. 'Help me' homework

Simply keeping going, or doing more, is a worthwhile if limited aim of homework, and getting pupils to keep going is hardly to be sniffed at. If the extension of lessons is to have other benefits, it is even better. In order to overcome some of the reasons teachers, never mind pupils, hate homework, a tremendously useful technique is to set homework that directly helps the teacher.

Pupils can help the teacher to plan, resource, teach, and assess lessons. As such help clearly involves some independent work by pupils, homework is in a good position to capture much of this kind of contribution. Examples of such work appear throughout this book. Here are a few simple activities by which pupils can be persuaded to complete homework and, best of all, help their teachers.

◆ A common way of recycling tests in **any subject**, and helping the teacher to make the most of the assessment opportunities offered by a test, is to set a test once in class (following a revision homework), and to set the test again for homework. Many teachers set this 're-test' only for pupils who have low marks. This seems a little unfair on those pupils with high marks (who deserve homework, too), and re-testing is always relevant for pupils with less than perfection in the first test. Perfect pupils can if necessary be set the supplementary homework of thinking of, and answering, three additional questions that could have been set in the test. Setting a test a second time also reduces the time the teacher spends preparing the homework. **(H4)**

◆ More interesting than merely setting a test (as in the previous section), a teacher can ask all the *pupils* to set a test. They are nearly always keen to think up questions for other people to answer, and a good homework would be to divide a topic up into sections, and get different pupils, or groups of pupils, to think up questions for each section. No one would then have an advantage in the resulting test.

 Ground rules are needed, so that questions are not impossible: perhaps saying that all the answers must be found in a certain book or set of books, or saying that the question-setters themselves will be responsible for justifying and feeding back on the questions they set. How better to exploit pupils' own competitiveness? **(L18)**

◆ Pupils completing work in class could, for homework, write an appropriate mark-scheme for that classwork. This encourages pupils to think about how they would like to be judged, and encourages teachers to 'trust' their pupils' homework, by using the best of the resulting mark schemes. They may even allow for pupils to mark each other's classwork, using their own mark schemes. **(H8)**

◆ Similar to a test, but easier to set, is the alphabet game. Write the letters of the alphabet down the side of a piece of paper, and fill in words starting with each letter. This can be adapted to suit any subject from **art** (names of artists, or art techniques or materials), to **zoology** (names of animals), and has been used by substitute teachers for years. The advantage of setting such a simple task for homework is that pupils are encouraged to do research from books, from other pupils and from teachers and family.

'Tell us about some famous women in history, sir', a puzzled **history** teacher was asked by a pupil previously thought to have been uninterested both in history and women. Later, the teacher caught up with the news of a wonderfully simple and clearly inspiring competition, run for the whole school, asking pupils to list as many famous women as possible. In such a way, pupils helped the whole staff review some of the gender issues across the curriculum.

Any homework that gets the pupils to analyse aspects of the school in this way will help teachers. Pupils might analyse school textbooks or corridor displays or the staff itself for representatives of different groups of people. Pupils are liable to 'get lost' in such work, spending far more time on it than expected. **(L7)**

◆ Other helpful (because re-usable) tasks include simple letter and word games, adaptable to different subjects, such as making anagrams of names or key words (my name becomes the cool and appropriate *just learnin'*), making up a sentence containing each of a list of key words (a game rather spoilt by its use in 1930s Europe to test for 'mental incapacity' and therefore suitability for extermination), or completing crosswords.

All these games can be fun, and with planning can make a valuable contribution to the **English/literacy** curriculum. It is easy, though, to set such tasks in a routine way, hoping that the fun will be justification enough. They should therefore be used with care, yet can be better than much hurriedly-set homework. **(H13)**

◆ Assessment is such an important part of the work of teachers, it is as well to make it more significant for pupils, and to engage pupils in self- and peer-assessment. This is at the heart of 'assessment for learning', the rebranded version of formative assessment. In some ways, completing self-assessment for homework can be risky: it is difficult enough being self-critical, without having to do it outside the classroom context. However, there are many self-assessment tasks that make for good homework, and good independent learning in general, as when pupils

- summarize all the work they have done that term,
- make a hierarchical list of the most important things they have learned, or
- choose and copy out the single piece of work they would most like to be remembered for, to be kept in a portfolio of the class's best work.

If parents are asked to counter-sign self-assessments by pupils, they may feel more creatively involved, especially prior to parents' evenings. Any contribution to assessment, by pupils or parents, will help teachers' workloads. **(H14)**

◆ The pupils could also be asked to pair up, and complete assessments of each other's work. (This works well for teachers, too, when they are asked to pair up and evaluate each other's teaching, rather than being 'appraised' by a manager.) Simply talking about work habits and achievements, outside the classroom, is justification enough for such homework tasks. If pupils are given the relevant syllabus attainment targets to work from, they may even get a better grasp than their teachers have of assessment, and be duly proud of their many achievements. **(L11)**

◆ As well as assessing their own and each other's work, pupils could evaluate a whole lesson. The teacher could ask a pupil or classroom assistant to describe the events of a lesson, in prose (as a description with timings down the side of the page) or diagrammatically (based on a map of the classroom with colour-coded ways of representing movement and talk). This description could be edited into a worksheet. For homework, get the pupils to analyse in writing what was happening, using appropriate criteria, perhaps even inspection criteria. This may have the added advantage of letting families know what goes on in the classroom.

◆ In the subsequent lesson, pupils can present extracts from their accounts. The descriptions and the evaluations based on them would, if sensitively edited, be ideal material for a parents' evening or open day exhibition, and for preparing departmental or school policies and for inspection visits by Ofsted. Parents may remember the work long after they have forgotten the rest of what their children did in school. **(L5)**

◆ Extending this idea, teachers who are concerned about an aspect of their professional life might gain the advice and support of pupils:

• A teacher concerned about how to help the class to concentrate better, could set the homework task 'How can this class be helped to concentrate better?'

- A teacher concerned about how to get through a syllabus in time for an exam might ask pupils to plan the remaining lessons in a way that could achieve their common aim.
- A teacher concerned at how education is under-valued, might even ask a class to justify a higher status (or in appropriate circumstances even higher pay) for teachers.

After a lesson in irony, teachers could set a homework task on why homework should be abolished. **(H20)**

◆ Pupils help each other and other pupils, for homework, by creating reference works such as dictionaries.

- A good task is to ask pupils to write explanations of words for younger pupils, for example setting a seven-word limit on the definition of each word, however complex that word is. By concentrating on words with which pupils are already familiar, the exercise can help pupils appreciate the difficulty of explanation; by concentrating on more difficult or technical words, the exercise can develop an improved vocabulary.
- A related exercise would be to get the pupils to make up new words, to match definitions you have given them; for example, a machine for measuring the level of brain activity in a classroom ('brainostopolist machine'? 'nousometer'?), the feeling you get when someone tells you a joke you have heard a hundred times ('groanopathy'?), the noise made when you push a spoon through the seal on a new jar of instant coffee ('jonjarvious'? 'scrrarp'?). The word 'quiz' is said, improbably, to have been invented as a result of a bet that the inventor could not introduce a new word into the language within a day. The bet was lost, as the word was scrawled on walls around Dublin overnight, and the next day had become a subject of conversation and lexicography. Perhaps pupils could come up with inventions as good as that one.

Writing dictionaries for younger pupils, incidentally, is helpfully 'inclusive' as well, and can be done for specialist vocabulary in **any subject**, as well as in **English** and in **MFL**. **(L20)**

◆ Extending the previous set of ideas, pupils might go on to develop mnemonics – acronyms made up of the first letters of a set of key concepts (one pupil came up with *SEWCLAWUCCA* to represent twentieth-century **history** encompassing suffrage, empires, World War One, communism, the League of Nations, Abyssinia, World War Two, the United Nations, cold war, computers and AIDS), or sentences (such as *Richard of York gave battle in vain*, for rainbows in **science**, or *I wish I could recollect of circle round, the exact relation Archimedes found*, for π in **maths**) having the same role. **(L4)**

◆ Further help might involve a homework activity for which each pupil has to produce one vital piece of information for a display, such as information related to a position on a controversial topic. In **RE**, a challenging topic for older pupils might be that of euthanasia, with each pupil being given a distinct website address, from a list created by the teacher (for example from the Religious Tolerance site at www.religioustolerance.org), and divided into three 'positions' ('pro', 'anti' and 'neutral').

The pupils should be briefed in the lesson on how to pick out the most important parts of a site in order to make a one-page summary of it. This summarizing activity could be practised for a single site in class, as a whole-class activity, but for homework each pupil will be responsible for a separate site. The resulting homework could be used for a large display, organized around the positions in the argument, to which all the pupils will have contributed. By individualizing the task for each pupil, teachers will be explicitly trusting all the pupils to make their individual contributions to the display, rather than giving the implicit message that only the best will be used. **(H7)**

◆ The help provided by pupils might not be for the teacher, but for the characters studied in class, whether figures important to **history** or **citizenship** education, authors of or characters from fiction in **English**, **artists** and **musicians**, **scientists** and inventors, or characters who speak the language studied in **MFL**. After studying any such people, the teacher could set the homework, on a prepared worksheet, of composing a letter to and from an 'agony aunt'.

The character's letter might begin 'Dear . . . , I am having a lot of troubles: no one seems to like me, and being a leader has caused so many problems, such as . . .', or 'Dear . . . , I am not sure how to paint a picture that represents how awful war can be in the twentieth century, . . .'. The agony aunt's letter might begin 'Dear . . . , This is what I would recommend . . .'. Working on the troubles of an important person can help pupils understand or even overcome some of their own worries. **(H5)**

◆ Finally, pupils might help themselves, which in turn could help the teacher. A well-established homework/research task, is to ask pupils to describe the three most recent or memorable ways they can remember that this subject in the school (or the school as a whole) helped them to feel positive about themselves. When teachers have set this task, they have often been surprised at what pupils come up with, and also the difficulties many pupils have, thinking of any ways in which the school made them feel good about themselves.

One teacher reported a pupil in a primary school who, after three years, could only come up with one example: 'The first day I was at school'. When asked why this was so memorable, he apparently replied 'Because I thought I could learn'. Teachers upset by such responses, or by their own, scant, memories of how their own schools made them feel good about themselves, have, in turn, used pupil responses to guide them in writing reports on pupils, and, more immediately, in giving enthusiastic, unqualified, positive and supportive feedback on the work completed. Real success is the success that can be remembered with pride. **(L11)**

3. 'Hammocking' homework

What stops teachers setting homework is rarely a belief that it is genuinely pointless, but a dislike of the hassle of setting, monitoring and assessing it. What can help? Setting interesting homework will of course help inspire the pupils. Yet some homework is never going to be exciting. In that case, teachers can try hammocking.

A hammock is a bed raised off the ground by two supports. In television, a potentially unpopular programme may lose the channel many viewers. When a channel has to broadcast such a programme, perhaps a charity appeal (to impress the licensing authorities) or a party political broadcast, they will usually try to 'hammock' it. They put a strong programme before and after the unpopular one, hoping that the strength of the programmes on either side will raise its viewing figures high enough to keep the channel from going broke. (According to www.ipsosmedia.com hammocking is simply 'maximising the audience to a weak programme by scheduling it between two strong programmes'.)

Homework can be similarly hammocked. A strong lesson either side of an unpopular homework can 'hold it up', as long as the lessons really do support the homework.

◆ Think of the worst homework in the world and see if it can be hammocked. A common choice as 'worst homework task' is to learn a list of words, either foreign vocabulary in **MFL**, technical words from a subject like **science**, **RE** or **geography**, or spellings in any subject. Hammocking can help.

- If the words are in another language, the first lesson might involve playing a record or an extract from a movie that included the words to be learnt; the homework, learn these words; the second lesson, play the record/movie again and translate it skilfully and enthusiastically.
- If the words are spellings, and the class is kind and supportive, the first lesson could involve giving back a set of previous work, and listing the misspelt words (taken from all the work); the homework, learn the correct spellings; second lesson, correct each other's work (that is why a kind class is needed), with points, credits or prizes, for the most spellings corrected.

A little competition of this form can make the time fly by that is spent on the most mundane task. **(H3)**

◆ Hammocking can be achieved by setting homework involving preparation for classwork. This is especially helpful when a series of lessons appears to be going nowhere, when the pupils and teacher alike are rather tiring of the topic. A final 'presentation lesson', perhaps a presentation to other pupils (in a year group assembly) or for a display, can liven up the most deadly of topics, and invigorate homework, in particular.

The stakes can be further raised (in turn, raising the hammock higher) if the presentation is announced as being one that will be tape-recorded. Oral work like this should also, at times, be formally assessed, so that pupils realize that the spoken word is as significant as the written word. In these circumstances, few will forget to bring their homework to school. **(H12)**

◆ Following up the 'presentation' work, a second homework might be to write a report on what happened in the presentation lesson (either their own part of the presentation, or the whole lesson), perhaps with the aim of making the reports into a display or permanent record of the presentation. This becomes a sort of double hammock, as the topic work, the presentation and the display, are like three trees between which are slung two homework tasks. It is also rather easy for the teacher to plan such linked-up homework. **(H4)**

◆ An interesting way of creating structure was suggested by an **English** teacher who commented on working in a room after another teacher. There was often a part of a poem left on the board (old technology: a blackboard), the ends of the lines hastily and inefficiently erased. The pupils were always more interested in the almost disappeared poem than in the work to be done in their own lesson. The teacher, therefore, took to writing a poem on the board himself, erasing half of it before the lesson started. When pupils said 'What is that about?', he could do a stunning lesson.

A good homework writing task, based on the paradox of the interest inspired by the disappearing poem, would be to give pupils a poem or piece of prose with the ends of lines erased. The more 'real' the erasing the better. Perhaps a daring teacher could get some very old, used, exercise books from the back of some cupboard, and tear a few pages in two, vertically, with a homework task being to complete the work. The task could be completed in any subject, involving a half-description of an experiment in **science**, a religious artefact in **RE**, or a product design in **technology**. Pupil curiosity is likely to overcome any mistrust of the teacher's intentions in setting homework. **(H10)**

◆ Creating plays, perhaps out of stories collected by pupils, provides opportunities for stimulating homework. Rehearsal is a popular homework in many ways, in **English** and in other subjects, as rehearsal involves a journey between a script or idea and a performance. It is a model of hammocking. Pupils may be willing to rehearse for hours to make a performance good, and will often take on many 'adult' characteristics, getting other pupils to work together, organizing props, being 'in charge'. Responsibility like this always helps homework, confounding the myths that pupils want simple, routine, homework, and that they cannot cooperate with each other. **(L20)**

◆ Other kinds of creation, in **design and technology**, can be hard to facilitate in homes, but if the investigation and design work can be completed for homework, it will be well hammocked by the manufacturing later completed in class. This can be continued by evaluation, completed later for homework. Evaluations are that much more significant if they involve a number of people, family or friends of the pupil, together evaluating a product. That the school is the place of manufacture, evaluated at home, helps demonstrate to all how important the school is, too. **(L10)**

◆ Key events can be described in class, and given in a jumbled form, for homework, to be re-ordered by the pupils. Events, in this sense, may be of many forms: historical events, stages of an experiment, elements of a piece of fiction in **English** or in **MFL** in another language. This can be quite a simple task, if pupils know a lot about the events. The format also lends itself to the development of high-level subject-based and logical skills.

Some textbooks provide pictures in the form of strip cartoons that, once re-ordered, can form the basis of such work. These 'jumbles' can also lead to effective extended writing. For almost a thousand years, the *Bayeux Tapestry* has no doubt been used in **history** lessons for such tasks. As pupils are puzzling, for homework, over materials given in class, the teacher has a kind of 'remote control' of pupils beyond the school. **(L8)**

◆ A related task might be to get pupils to produce, between them, an effective narrative display, modelled on a strip cartoon or a medieval **religious** narrative painting. Each pupil or group of pupils might be given one element of a narrative, and the homework task would be hammocked by the need for a complete narrative in the following lesson: a memorable conclusion to the homework. **(L4)**

◆ Where a lot of information is to be absorbed, homework could involve preparation for a demanding class activity. Having given out information about different elements to be learned (for homework), the hammocking can be achieved by the next lesson including a number of scenarios in which knowledge of the elements is vital.

For example, in **geography** the pupils might be given descriptions of different factors affecting climate, such as air pressure, wind patterns, topography, distance from the equator, and the effects of human interventions such as 'greenhouse gases', deforestation, and diverting or damming rivers.

The scenarios to be developed in the next lesson could be of the form 'I am a farmer in Bengal; what climate changes would I fear the most, and what could help my situation?' or 'I live in Tokyo and have a chance to address the United Nations on climate change; what should I speak about?' The pupils would have to 'solve' each scene as effectively as possible, and justify their choice to the rest of the group. Teachers will be as keen to hear the solutions as pupils will be to provide them. **(H8)**

◆ Questions can be prepared, for homework, to be used in a role-played interview in the next class. Pupils may be asked to prepare three questions to be asked of **religious** figures at decisive moments in their lives, **historical** figures prior to key events, **literary** figures after having written the material being studied, witnesses to earthquakes or floods for **geography**, or **sporting** figures preparing for a competition. It is helpful if a few (better and worse) questions are discussed in class as examples, before the homework, so that pupils can understand the advantages of asking more open questions, and so that their conversational skills can be better developed. **(L2)**

This chapter has described various ways of expanding the learning time of pupils, by keeping them going on otherwise boring tasks, encouraging pupils to help teachers, and lifting up all tasks by hammocking them. It is in these ways that pupils and teachers can all solve the 'time' problems usually suffered by homework. Making homework more stimulating, less worrisome, and more helpful for teachers, the whole school will benefit. Teachers may even stop campaigning for the abolition of homework **(H20)**, although there is plenty more work to be done, in this book, to address all the arguments for abolition.

2 Application homework: making school subjects important

Homework in this chapter

School is relevant, isn't it?

The school curriculum is important. Teachers teach subjects they think are important, and however narrow some syllabuses might be, there have to be ways in which the subjects can be made to seem important to pupils. If school subjects have any currency beyond the school, then homework can help their importance be better understood. Homework can carry the subjects out into the world beyond the school, with the time spent on homework being used to apply school work to that world. Indeed, several good homework tasks can be set about the importance of subjects themselves, or of topics within subjects.

◆ For the subject taught, find an authoritative description of the subject or a topic within it. The description may come from key texts in the area, or, for National Curriculum subjects, from QCA guidance (the 'importance of the subject' descriptions are currently hidden away in www.nc.uk.net and click on 'download national curriculum booklets'). The homework task can be to describe five ways in which the subject, as described, could be of value to the pupils outside their school lives.

Music, for example, is described as a subject that 'brings together intellect and feeling and enables personal expression, reflection and emotional development' that 'helps pupils understand themselves and relate to others, forging important links between the home, school and the wider world'. Pupils could describe ways in which the subject, as taught, might help them do this, or they could review the regularity (daily, weekly, yearly) with which the subject, or their lives outside school, exemplifies these aims. **(H10)**

Among the ways in which homework can apply classwork to the outside world, some are related to becoming a kind of apprentice member of a 'subject-related' world (becoming an archivist, a chemist, a footballer), some are related to the often passive, 'couch potato', lifestyle led by many young people and quite a few old people, and some are related to more active 'wandering about' activities that young and old may enjoy.

1. 'Apprenticeship' homework

All learning can be described as a kind of apprenticeship. A whole discipline has grown up in education psychology around what is called 'situated learning', saying that learning typically takes place when a person becomes a participant, initially quite a peripheral participant, in a social activity, and gradually becomes more central to that activity. Examples include work-based apprenticeships but also other family and friendship groups. Writers such as Wenger who promote this approach sometimes criticize school learning, because it does not involve taking part in a real social activity, other than the social activity of school itself: 'school learning is just learning school' (Wenger 1998). Homework may be able to convert some of this 'learning school' into real learning, by relating subject disciplines to social activities beyond the school.

Food technology can be made more about being an apprentice in the narrow field of catering, or the broader field of cookery, for example, and **history** can be made more about being an apprentice archivist, or the broader field of historically aware person. The '21st century **science**' project (www.21stcenturyscience.org) is a neat rebranding of seventeenth-century scientific ideas, promoting the idea of developing the 'scientific literacy' that pupils need 'to play a full part in a modern democratic society', but also, for some students 'producing courses which provide the first stages of their training as a scientist, or for a career that involves science'.

Scientific literacy is itself a broad kind of apprenticeship (being an apprentice member of a 'modern democratic society'), with the narrower apprenticeship being in science-related careers. This combination of broad and narrow apprenticeships is also to be found in subjects such as **RE** (broad religious literacy for all, and authentic understanding of ways of life that a narrower group of pupils might follow), **English** (broad literacy, narrow 'creative writing' perhaps), and **PE** (healthy living for all, elite sport). Here are some broad or narrow apprenticeship homework tasks.

◆ The act of production motivates pupils. They may spend hours working on a picture, playing an instrument, constructing a model, planning and making a meal, even if it has nothing to do with school. Such practical work is therefore ideal for homework, yet the obvious problem is that most homes are not equipped for the whole range of such practical work. Several schools overcome this problem by getting pupils to do homework in school: lunchtime choirs or bands for **music**, after-school **art** clubs, producing food for a parents' evening complementing **food technology**.

This seems a good way of approaching homework, and a good use of school resources, if staffing issues are sorted out first. Yet some form of food preparation is done in every home, so carefully arranged homework tasks involving planning and preparing meals should be possible, whatever equipment and materials are available.

Flexibility is needed, so pupils can match their work to their circumstances. And reporting back on the events of the home-meal should prove helpful for classwork, especially evaluative work, building on the evaluations no doubt offered by other family members. **(L5)**

◆ In **history**, understanding often comes with comparison, and work for homework is helpful when it involves comparing the history being studied to a familiar aspect of the pupils' lives. For example:

- follow work on the myths of the foundation of Rome with a homework asking pupils to make up legend on foundation of their home town, or to make up another twins legend; or
- after working on the good and bad qualities of Louis XVI and/or Marie Antoinette as leaders, get the pupils, for homework, to do a similar list of the good and bad qualities of a recent or current British prime minister as a leader.

Pupils should be ready to argue for their choices, perhaps at home and with friends, and certainly in class. **(L3)**

◆ Similarly narrow 'historian' apprenticeship work, after work on the diary of Anne Frank, would ask pupils to write their own diaries for a week, just covering what happens in school. With the pupils' permission, and working in supportive groups in class, pupils could analyse the validity and bias in other pupils' diaries, as a way of assessing the use of diaries by historians. Writing diary entries is itself a good way of developing regular work habits, and hence taking control of deadlines. **(L15)**

◆ Popular **history** homework tasks include letters home from and to the trenches of the First World War. It may be useful to set a series of homework tasks, interspersed with other tasks, so that pupils create a set of three or four pairs of letters, from and to different war arenas, and at different stages of the war. The pupils often get more and more historically sophisticated as the series goes on, in part in response to the quality of the teacher's comments on each set of letters as it is submitted.

A series of letters can itself become an extended historical narrative, and other related work might include letters to newspapers, trying to stop the war at an early stage, or a letter from the Kaiser, asking for clemency after the war. In such ways, pupils are becoming apprentice 'people in and of history'. This in turn helps them develop critical **PSHE** skills, enabling pupils to understand their own roles as citizens, to the great pleasure of their teachers. **(L6)**

◆ More direct apprenticeship homework for **citizenship** would be the setting up of a school council, participation in which could take up a considerable amount of energy and imagination of pupils. School Councils UK (www.schoolcouncils.org) says it would improve academic performance, life skills, and teacher–pupil relations, and reduce bullying. School can hardly teach 'about' democracy without having something like a school council. Allowing councillors to count this as homework adds to its value, and the value of homework itself as an enrichment of the curriculum. **(L16)**

◆ In **science**, narrow apprenticeships as biologists might include homework tasks such as reviewing plant species in the school grounds or in the environment around pupils' homes. This could be developed into broader 'scientific literacy' work when tied in to an environmental issue such as the effects of pollution or funding cuts on such plant life. The environment is always there, to be exploited for such homework tasks. **(L17)**

◆ **RE** teachers are often, rightly, wary of the idea that RE tries to make people religious, but they cannot avoid looking at why people are, or are not, religious. Broader religious literacy can easily be exemplified in the homework task of finding two people to talk to who have different views on a religious topic being studied in RE. If worship is being studied, the conversations might be with someone who thinks worship is very important to them and someone who thinks it is not important.

◆ Any such conversation will also be helpful for pupils in clarifying their own positions on such issues, and is therefore able to support narrower apprenticeships in 'living a religious or non-religious life'. Other tasks might be to plan for a birth ceremony or a wedding of someone from a specified religious tradition. People are the resources used for these activities, and pupils who may have difficulty talking about the issues with people at home might be encouraged to ask people in the school, instead. **(L18)**

◆ A rather more sinister and enjoyable **RE** apprenticeship task is to ask the pupils to imagine that religion has been made illegal, and they have all been recruited to the 'religion police'. They must, for homework, spot all evidence of religion between this lesson and the next week's lesson. Evidence might include:

- religious symbols worn by people, whether worn for religious reasons or simply as jewellery,
- religious buildings,
- indications on shops, such as 'ideal for Christmas', or 'Halal meat',
- conversations in which people use religious terms, including 'Bless you', or
- television programmes mentioning religion.

Pupils engage imaginatively in the exercise, many showing a frightening affinity for police work of this kind, and RE teachers are as likely to fear the completion, rather than the absence, of the homework. **(H16)**

◆ For **MFL**, if homework is effective, then the teachers have already succeeded in their hardest task: getting pupils to use their new language skills outside the classroom. Next stop, Paris. The availability of current foreign language text and video, through the internet and digital television, makes a range of apprenticeship homework tasks possible.

Reporting back to the class on that day's news, from an online French newspaper (e.g. from www.onlinenewspapers.com/), or planning a Spanish holiday using a Spanish language guide such as those from the local paper in Ibiza (www.diariodeibiza.es/). Homework is more like entertainment than punishment. **(H18)**

◆ Similarly, it is not difficult to plan **English** homework tasks with both broad and narrow apprenticeships. Just as setting a test may be more educative and inspiring than merely taking a test, pupils teaching English may be more educative than merely being taught English. Homework can be used to prepare work to be completed with younger pupils, either supporting the teacher or making a presentation.

The experience of explaining work is often inspirational, and is certainly likely to increase the sympathy with which pupils regard their teachers. Literacy and literary work with younger pupils can be justified for all pupils:

- those of considerable ability, who find their own work rather too easy, can be challenged by work that would otherwise be regarded as 'beneath them',
- those with learning difficulties can have a good 'excuse' to work on more basic tasks,
- those with challenging behaviour are often the best at keeping order when teaching.

Pupils can plan work in teams, and through evaluating the activities of the pupils, they may themselves learn more about the assessment of their own English work. Making pupils into teachers, teachers are making themselves redundant, in the nicest possible sense. **(L12)**

◆ A piece of creative work illustrating a narrow apprenticeship, in **English** or **art** or **music**, needs brave teachers. The teachers take examples of their own creative writing, art or composition, and give them to their pupils, uncredited. Set the homework task of analysing, interpreting and critically evaluating the work. This should be done as homework to minimize the opportunity for pupils to ask about the poem and its author. The pupils should report back in the next lesson.

Teachers courageous enough to set this task find that pupils come up with meanings and interpretations that had never occurred to them, the creator of the work. Once the authorship is revealed, the pupils will want to ask about the piece, and will want to know that their interpretations were significant whether or not the creator had thought of them.

This homework task becomes an apprenticeship, when the pupils are set a creative task of a similar kind, for their next homework. Their creations should in turn be submitted for analysis and critical review by other pupils. In order to create the best conditions for fair critique, it might be best if the critique is completed by pairs: pairs of pupils swapping pieces of work for analysis, talking to each other in a supportive situation. **(L2)**

◆ Pupils could be described as apprentice people: learning how communities and society works, developing into adults with full citizenship rights. One of the pleasant surprises of the **citizenship** curriculum, as it was published in 2000, was the requirement that pupils be 'developing skills of participation and responsible action'. This was an extension to the knowledge and understanding that might have been expected.

If pupils are to participate, this will be both in school and outside school, or as the curriculum describes it, they should 'negotiate, decide and take part responsibly in both school and community-based activities' (www.nc.uk.net). This is one of the most powerful curriculum-based incentives to set good homework tasks. Some schools see this element of the citizenship curriculum as simply requiring audit: asking pupils about their community-based activities. Other schools are more active, and set up opportunities to take part in such activities, and this is more like a form of homework.

Community-based activities can of course be controversial, and it is still unclear how schools may react to pupils taking a full and active role in political activities and controversial campaigns that might not fit the school's image of the 'respectable citizen'. Should pupils be supported by their schools in campaigns involving civil disobedience? Should the citizenship activities of pupils only be recognized by the school if they are politically mainstream, and fit with the school's policies, or can more controversial political activity (of the extreme right or the extreme left, for example) still count towards meeting the citizenship curriculum? Or does the word 'responsibly' in the phrase 'take part responsibly' simply mean 'as the teachers would prefer'?

Teachers and pupils can argue about these issues in citizenship lessons, and the homework arising naturally from the arguments will be true apprenticeships in life as citizens. Students from Hull set up an online political television station to engage young people (Catch21, at www.catch21.co.uk/), and this may help continue the debate. **(L3)**

♦ As pupils grow up, they are developing physically and emotionally. **PE** and **PSHE** both address these developments in school, and both hope to address them out of school as well. It is a good advert for homework, if PE and PSHE homework is viable and effective.

In both subjects, more individualized coaching and mentoring can be available outside lessons. For PE, the coaching may be elite sports coaching, or in the style of a 'personal trainer'. For PSHE, the mentoring may be in lunchtime, after-school or holiday clubs, trying to tip the pupils over to a higher grade, or it may be related to special educational needs, the gifted and talented, gender or ethnicity.

Whether or not these activities are called 'homework', they are homework. Teachers welcome reports on such work, from the coaches or mentors, and are usually more enthusiastic about these kinds of apprenticeships than much of the rest of out-of-class work. **(H8)**

♦ The natural follow-up to the previous exercise, is to ask pupils themselves to coach and mentor younger pupils, individually or for tournaments or other collaborative events. Groups of 14-year-old pupils, themselves trained in aspects of healthy living (whether diet, road safety or exercise), can develop for homework a 'lesson' to be taught to 7-year-olds.

The prospect of being faced with a class of young children is generally more than enough to encourage the completion of the homework. Pupils working as apprentice teachers, in this way, develop a keen sense of the hard work put in by their own teachers. **(H12)**

2. 'Couch potato' homework

An old saying suggests that you know you are old when, if you fall down, you wonder what else you can do while you are down there. In the same way, for school pupils, although it is not a good idea to promote the idea of being a 'couch potato', it may be a good idea to promote ways of making couch potatoing more educative.

Many teachers feel they are unable to get their pupils to do enough homework because the pupils watch too much television. (A survey done in the 1930s said much the same about the effects of radio.)

One solution would be to set 'Watch the television' as homework. It would help if the programme was relevant to the subject being taught, but imaginative teachers could probably find a task that could involve watching almost anything.

◆ Why might a **maths** teacher ask pupils to watch a music channel? Perhaps to estimate favoured camera angles.

◆ Why might an **RE** teacher ask pupils to watch a football match? Perhaps to analyse heroism, adulation and charismatic power.

There are also straightforward couch-based tasks such as watching television sport as the basis for pupils to write reviews of matches or competitions. **(H2)**

◆ Two ways of making good use of television are helping pupils decide *what* they watch, and helping them change *how* they watch. On any evening, there will be programmes on topics that will benefit pupils' education. The news, of course, helps with many subjects, especially **English** and **citizenship**, but there will also be programmes relevant to most subjects.

It may not be the best advert for a programme to say 'This will help you with school work', so programme makers may hide the obvious relevance of their products. The teacher and pupils could, in a lesson, plan what to watch in the following week, of relevance to that subject. They could also develop 'how' to watch television: how to spot scientific absurdities in science fiction, sociologically inaccurate patterns in soap operas, anachronisms in historical dramas, and biases and political propaganda in almost any programme.

Watching television critically is a life skill of enormous benefit, and this idea is followed up in some other suggestions in this section of the book, helping make life in general, and being a couch potato in particular, a little less boring. **(L13)**

◆ One simple homework task has proved popular in **RE**, when studying religious moral rules such as the Ten Commandments of Jewish and Christian traditions or the Five Precepts of Buddhism. Pupils are asked to watch an episode of a soap opera, and analyse who breaks each of the rules, and what the consequences are of each transgression.

Not only can pupils come to understand the moral rules and the rules of soap operas (where sins are usually punished at the end of an episode), but they can also exemplify sloth (one of the Seven Deadly Sins) whilst completing their homework. Parents may even be convinced that the world has gone mad, as they tell their children 'No, just sit there and watch *EastEnders*, like your teacher says'. **(H17)**

◆ Still sitting on the couch, pupils can practise talking. A phrase can be said in many different ways. 'I'm doing my homework now' could be said angrily, sadly, cheerfully, cynically, obsequiously, pompously and so on. Set the **English** or **drama** homework task of practising saying this phrase in each of these ways.

The homework can be well hammocked, as pupils enjoy coming up with other adverbs to add to the list given them, and may enjoy hearing their teachers trying to say the phrase in a couple of the ways themselves. In the follow-up lesson, the pupils can work in pairs to test out their skill at speaking in these ways, with the partner practising their listening skills by trying to guess the adverb being illustrated. **(L2)**

◆ What are the most common words (or the most common verbs, or the most common words with more than three syllables, etc.) in use? Brainstorm for the ones pupils think are most common (presumably excluding offensive words), and write a list of the six favourites. For homework, get the pupils to listen carefully, for 30 minutes or an hour, to conversations (or television programmes, if the topic suits), and tick off the number of times each word is used.

Feed back the results in the next lesson. Perhaps different groups of pupils could record conversations in different situations, some during mealtime, some when young people are talking amongst themselves, some in a shop and so on. Pupils' real lives can be celebrated by such homework. **(L14)**

◆ Other listening tasks include the very simple one: what has just been said? Some people have difficulty remembering what has been said on a weather forecast, or in a news bulletin, or in a film. Pupils could ask other members of the family what has just been said (on television, or perhaps in a conversation), to see how people's memories work.

They might instead be asked to listen very carefully, just the once, to a particular piece of dialogue (for example, the first two minutes of a soap opera), and report back in the class the next day about what exactly was said. Adding the rule that no writing must be done, adds to the difficulty and to the attractiveness of this rather competitive homework activity. Pupils who listen carefully may also be further encouraged in this by their families. **(L19)**

◆ Someone once said that since leaving school, the only thing he had read was a box of corn flakes. He may be surprised to learn that there are almost a thousand words on a typical corn flakes packet. As a homework, get pupils to read something that is not usually thought of as 'real' reading, to be reported on in the next lesson. Cereal packets could work well, as could all the words of shop signs in the local high street, or the printed words appearing in television adverts (another surprisingly high total), or the signs or notices inside a car or bus.

By making pupils read what they might otherwise fail to bother about, they can be made more aware of the variety of styles used in different contexts. Teachers, too, admit with this homework that school books are not the only reading relevant to pupils' education. **(L9)**

◆ Pupils could be asked to daydream, working out how to spend a £9 million windfall (a lottery win, or a lottery grant, say), backing up their daydream by finding accurate prices from paper or online catalogues and newspaper adverts.

The task could be made more specific to a subject such as **geography** (restricting the money spent to flood relief, or environmental improvement), or **science** (restricting the money spent to scientific equipment needed to improve the school laboratories). The results would make a wonderful display, with idle daydreams being made into **mathematically**, geographically, scientifically inspiring plans. **(H2)**

◆ Couch-based homework tasks could include working out and the relationship between food consumption and age, or between gender and preferences for television programmes, or political views of parents and children. As with the lottery homework tasks, these can be used to help develop calculation skills (useful in **maths**) and their application to particular subjects, in these cases, presumably, **food technology**, **PSHE** and **citizenship**.

In even more idle moments, people have been known to count repeated objects: a flower pattern on wallpaper, ceiling tiles, bricks in a wall. Large-number homework tasks might estimate the number of bricks used to build the school, or the town, or all the buildings in the world. 'Averages' work could be completed watching the television: pupils might work out the mean age of characters in different soap operas, as some are 'older' than others, or the modal number of 'cuts' in a 30-second advert. Even boring shows can become interesting. **(L13)**

◆ Couches and chairs can themselves be investigated for homework, with the range of their uses in homes and school, and their symbolic uses, such as thrones or 'chairs' of meetings, forming the basis for further book-based research, too. Items from around the house have always been popular with **design and technology** teachers, whether looking at kettles, window locks, mugs, or items of clothing or jewellery.

Pupils can study them to get ideas for class work, or to look for more subtle distinctions such as the difference between incrementally and radically changed styles. Realizing that their own lives at home are worth studying, pupils will appreciate how homework makes sense for them as individuals. **(L14)**

◆ Still on the couch, but with a hot drink, pupils might be asked to make a hot drink and carefully time and estimate the heat changes and transfers, including the cooling of the liquid, the heating and cooling of the mug and spoon, and the warming of the surface on which the mug is standing. More accurate measurements could then be completed in a school **science** laboratory. Related work on heat insulation could be applied to thermos flasks or pizza boxes. The simplest objects of the home become objects of serious study. **(L17)**

◆ Staying with **science**, but going back to more contemplative idleness, pupils could be asked to wonder: to wonder, without recourse to books or conversation, about topics relevant to different subjects.

- Why do animals huddle?
- Why do both eyes blink at the same time (a real evolutionary puzzle, this one)?
- As sliding down a stair banister is so much easier than climbing up one, why is it just as hard walking down stairs as climbing up them?
- Why do people have eyebrows?
- Why are cartoon characters so often drawn with big heads?
- Why does a pencil, waved up and down in front of a television, 'flash', and flash more quickly when going up than down?
- What if we did not have elbows (the title of a recent book for children)?
- What if gravity were reduced?
- What if you only had food to the value of 300 calories a day (the common diet in concentration camps)?
- What if the world's temperature increased by two or three degrees?
- What if H_2O became consistently more dense as its temperature lowered, that is, what if ice did not float?

Once convinced of the value of thinking in this way, pupils can become lost in such contemplation. **(L7)**

◆ More complex 'thinking' problems could be on the work done by a superhero. How much energy would it take to stop a speeding train with your hands, while standing on the sleepers, or what temperature would your breath have to be to 'freeze' a villain?

Not only could pupils try to solve such problems, while on the couch, they could also think up other similar superhero **physics** problems, entertaining other pupils and even their teachers. **(L6)**

◆ Complex thinking in **history**, from the couch, might follow classwork on bias in accounts of the characters of Richard III, participants in the Gunpowder Plot, or the Suffragettes. Pupils could be asked to cut articles out of newspapers or magazines, or video television news reports, that they think are biased, to be described to the class in the next lesson.

The same could be completed on the topic of propaganda, an issue all too often confused with bias. If pupils are unable to find examples of bias or propaganda in their everyday lives, they have much to learn in history. If they do find such examples, they will have a skill for life. **(L1)**

◆ During a popular international event, such as the Olympics or World Cup, **geography** or **PE** teachers could ask the pupils to watch the events (which is not usually difficult), and, having assigned particular countries to individual pupils or groups of pupils, they could be asked find out at least two facts about 'their' country.

Pupils might be required to get their information entirely from the television or internet coverage, which is particularly easy to organize, or, perhaps for a second homework task, they might be allowed to use other reference texts. **(H11)**

◆ Contemplate. The idea of asking pupils to do (almost) nothing for homework is particularly attractive: a silence or 'nothingness' of great significance. Either in **PE** or **RE**, pupils could be trained in appropriate ways to clear their minds and calmly relax their bodies. It is easy to joke about such tasks, as idleness can have many harmful consequences. Yet young people (like old people) often have no time for genuinely calm and undistracted contemplation. Their idleness is too often dominated by distraction and stress or worry. **(H19)**

3. 'Wandering about' homework

Having contemplated, perhaps pupils can be asked to complete homework while a little more active. Some of the suggested tasks involve wandering around inside or outside the home, some involve more metaphorical wandering, book-based or virtual. Teachers may themselves enjoy using wandering about in lessons, and there is a well-known theory of education leadership called 'school management by wandering around' (Frase and Hetzel 1990).

◆ Starting with some virtual wandering, pupils may be encouraged to 'wander' through quite difficult texts, when set a task of choosing the three sentences, or lines, that they most and least enjoyed, justifying their choices.

Focused web wandering can be encouraged through what are

known as 'webquests' (explained and exemplified at WebQuest. org), which can apply to any subject. In **RE**, for example, individual pupils, or small groups, may be given particular website addresses, on different religious views of the environment, and asked to summarize and evaluate them, coming back to class with material that can be combined and contrasted. Once the pattern has been set, webquest homework tasks are easy to organize and are remarkably productive. **(H11)**

♦ The most popular form of virtual wandering, long pre-dating computers, is dreaming, either daydreaming (on a couch?) or dreaming at night. Asking pupils to fall asleep for homework has a certain appeal. There are many guides to dream analysis. In **PSHE** lessons, teachers might use any of a number of more or less convincing guides, to develop pupils' abilities to understand themselves and others.

A rule must be, of course, that the pupils choose which dreams to report to the class, and which to keep to themselves. This also requires telling pupils in advance what kinds of meanings there might be, so that pupils are not unnecessarily embarrassed by the subsequent interpretation of the dream. Meanwhile, no pupil can complain of having lost sleep over their homework. **(H1)**

♦ Moving very little from the couch, but with at least some opportunity to wander around, pupils could be asked for **science** to experiment on themselves by testing their pulse rates on the hour every hour for 12 hours, listing (with appropriate propriety) what they were doing at each time. Pupils will find out how they live, and how they might live more or less healthily, with such a task. **(L16)**

♦ To engage with pupils' homes, there are many activities that help pupils get a sense of building-based numbers. Simply getting pupils looking around their homes, as part of homework, will increase the chances of it being done. **Mathematical** calculations could be of the form

- multiply the number of windows by the number of doors, then divide by the number of rooms, or
- find and sketch examples from your home of angles of 90°, 60°, 45°.

More complex house-based work would be the calculation of the proportions of rooms, or average floor space, to be analysed in class, perhaps, looking at the patterns of room function and room proportions or floor area. Care must be taken to avoid embarrassing pupils coming from very small or very large houses. Answers that do not give away evidence of wealth or poverty are always to be preferred, so that homework adds to pupils' curiosity, not embarrassment, about their homes. **(H6)**

◆ The house is full of measurement scales: degrees on ovens and central heating systems, energy on food packets, frequency on radios. Pupils could be asked to complete a survey of all the measurement scales used in their homes, with pupils competing to find the most, or the most unusual, scales. (A flood-level post, marked in fathoms, is the most unusual scale found in past settings of this homework task.) The real lives of pupils can be studied in such apparently 'technical' **science** tasks. **(L16)**

◆ Other **science** house surveys might include:

- house plants in and around the house,
- minibeasts in and around the house,
- pets in the house and neighbourhood,
- the uses of plastics, or wood, or other materials,
- sounds in the home, for example of road traffic, aircraft, neighbours talking, television and radio, bird song, heating systems, creaking floorboards, lifts, wind, kettles, and all the sounds made by people and pets.

Teacher curiosity helps make such work that much more enjoyable for pupils. **(H7)**

◆ House-based tasks can encourage pupils to take responsibility in various ways. There are **design** tasks for products suitable for disabled as well as able-bodied people. Pupils of all abilities (and especially those with sensory impairments) are likely to be interested to know, for example, that a famous 'range' cooker was designed by a man who was blind. Designing other kitchen equipment for the visually impaired is a challenging task. Based on the cooker example, pupils should be able, too, to think about how disabled people might themselves design products. Pupil achievements in these tasks will be especially pleasing for them. **(L11)**

◆ A home is likely to contain products and materials from all around the world. Pupils could survey such sources, in preparation for work on trade routes or interdependence. Contributing to the home, pupils could be asked for **MFL** to make labels for objects around the house, in French, German, Spanish or any mother-tongue.

This is an entertaining activity, as pupils generally insist on using humour, such as labelling a sibling's door with a foreign-language description that is less than complimentary. Many years later, when travelling abroad, adults still remember these simple labels. **(L1)**

◆ There are many possible uses in **art** of the photographs collected in most homes, if families give their permission (an important ethical consideration), and photographic collages are much easier to produce with digital cameras.

Either the original copies, or, preferably, duplicates, of photographs of the pupil could be put together into a composite portrait, in the style of David Hockney's work. A whole room can be pictured, with the pictures made up of close-up shots of different elements digitally 'stitched'.

Hockney was concerned, in his photographic work, to show many views of the same person or scene (search for 'hockney photography' at images.google.co.uk). It is such multi-perspective work that made his choice of photography so interesting. Before Hockney, Cubists had done similar work, as had medieval religious painting, with later portraits, such as those done of the Elizabethans, often being more subtle collections of perspectives, with meaningful views out of windows and significant objects left 'casually' on tables in the background. Teachers, let alone pupils, will be fascinated. **(H14)**

◆ Wandering beyond the home, shopping exercises have always been popular, and homework could be set asking pupils to act as mathematical shopping advisers to friends or families. Surveys of prices calculating average shopping baskets, or work on petrol prices, could be useful. Pupils could provide a consumer advice service to others in the school, and in such ways link with **food technology** and **business studies**. Those who benefit from the advice will appreciate the value of homework. **(H17)**

◆ One correspondent tells me that her own personal favourite piece of homework, remembered decades after it was set, was some work in **geography** researching the places fruit came from. 'I can remember going to the greengrocers and collecting the tissue wrappers that fruit used to be wrapped in, which had beautiful designs on them and smelled delicious. Then I looked up in an atlas where they came from (no computers then!) and found out about the countries from reference books'. Smelly homework: now there's a title for another book. **(L4)**

◆ Maps and other scale drawings can be set as homework tasks, and these may link **geography**, **maths** and **art** work. Maps of journeys to and from school, and scale drawings of objects or pictures found in the home, are generally engaging. Extending such work, pupils could produce plans for local environmental improvements, designing new street furniture or shop signs, developed in conversation with friends and family members who are likely, themselves, to have strong views on such matters. **(L19)**

◆ A further development can be that much more controversial. Building shops or houses in an area will often cause intense local arguments. Pupils in **geography** can be given a list of six-figure coordinates in the locality, and for homework can justify siting houses or shops on one of those sites, having argued through the preferences with family and friends. **(L3)**

◆ The school can be wandered about, too. School prospectuses and websites, and the details of school design (such as signposts and displays), are noticed by pupils and can be analysed and developed by pupils, for homework.

Skills in marketing, as well as in critical analysis, can be developed if pupils question their own families and fellow pupils about how the school and its publicity material compares with other schools and their materials. 'Making the school even better' could be a topic in **citizenship**, **art**, **PSHE**, **design and technology**, or all four subjects. Few pupils will hold back from making suggestions about improving their own school, so homework will be handed in with pleasure. **(H12)**

By applying classwork to the world beyond the classroom, home-work can make school subjects that much more important, building up greater trust between teachers, pupils and their families. Whether becoming apprentice archivists or apprentice human beings, the most couch-potatoed pupil can learn, and even wander about, carry-ing their classwork into the years to come.

Just as parents never stop feeling responsible for and worrying about their children, even when their children are grown up with families of their own, teachers can use 'application' homework to ensure they are responsible for school-learning being taken by pupils into the rest of their lives. This is what teachers can give to the world. What they can take from the world, is the subject of the next chapter.

Capture homework: bringing the world into the classroom

Homework in this chapter

'Inclusion' homework	All subjects	82
	Art	80–1
	Citizenship	77
	Design and technology	79–80
	English	80–1, 82
	Geography	77, 78
	History	73, 78–9
	Maths	76–7, 79
	Music	80
	PSHE	73, 77–8, 81–2
	RE	73, 77–8, 80–1, 82
	Science	82

There's a world out there, isn't there?

It should not need saying, but the world beyond the classroom is a full and fascinating place, rich in life and talk and stimulation of every kind, good and bad. If pupils to the age of 16 spend something like 125,000 hours out of school, can we not exploit some of that time?

Instead of homework being the vehicle for applying 15,000 hours of classwork to the world (as in Chapter 2), it can instead be the vehicle for capturing the world for it to be used in class. There must be a degree of trust between pupils, teachers and families, for this to work. Teachers cannot pretend to be the only people to contribute to the curriculum, despite their considerable subject-specialist knowledge and professional skills. However, the rewards, if trust is gained, are enormous.

Education can become a part of life, not an escape from it, and a part of life that explains and enhances the whole experience. This is the model of school-as-community that is well expressed by the philosopher Macmurray (1968, 1991), for whom the school is a 'broadened' family as 'education . . . is the means of extending the spirit of the family beyond its boundaries to the society as a whole'. Macmurray says that in schools teachers 'are not training children to be mathematicians or accountants or teachers or linguists', they 'are training them to be men and women, to live human lives properly' and 'to be educated today means to have learned to be human – not Scottish, not British, not even West-European – but human'. If the 'golden aim' of education is 'to teach the children how to live', this should not be 'crowded out by a multiplicity of little aims'.

'Capture' homework therefore sees school as partly deriving from non-school life, especially home life. It recognizes that schooling is primarily about humanity: the 'apprenticeship' is an apprenticeship in humanity, and subjects are there in order to contribute to the humanity, to the social, moral, spiritual and cultural development of pupils. This is stated, in various curriculum documents.

History, for example, helps pupils to 'see the diversity of human experience, and understand more about themselves as individuals and members of society', **maths** 'equips pupils with a uniquely powerful set of tools to understand and change the world', and **design and technology** helps makes pupils 'autonomous and creative problem solvers, as individuals and members of a team' (all from the www.nc.uk.net). 'Capture' homework means that teachers should not be seeking the help of parents and other members of the community; they should be seeking partnership. It is worth quoting the four principles used in the book *Involving Parents* (Stern 2003), as these are most important when applied to this form of homework:

- School is about the whole of life, and teachers need to draw on the outside world, including the world of pupils' families.

- The curriculum should be applicable to the rest of pupils' lives. The curriculum is not for the benefit of the subjects, it is for the benefit of the pupils. It should help them understand, grow, take hold of the world, become more 'real'.

- Parents know more than teachers about their children, and are likely to have taught them more, too.

- Parents are not cheap substitutes for teachers: teachers are, at best, quite expensive substitutes for parents.

Schools have been setting 'capture' homework for many years, for example through the 'show and tell' activity popular with primary schools when a pupil brings something interesting from home, to describe to the rest of the class. Three kinds of homework of this sort are described here.

◆ Chat shows exploit the interest in and motivation to take part in discussions and arguments, and to record those discussions: 'chat show' homework does the same.

◆ Hobbies are activities people do for their own individual interest or amusement: 'hobby' homework attempts to capture some of that interest for use in school.

◆ Whereas hobbies and associated homework reflect individual interests, 'inclusion' homework tasks try to capture something of the communal life of pupils beyond the classroom.

1. 'Chat show' homework

Talking is good for learning, even if pupils can go through more than a decade of schooling thinking that to talk in school is a sin. Talking tasks make for good homework, as pupils can find ways to talk, outside class, even when writing is something of a challenge.

◆ The simplest form of homework of this kind is to ask the pupils to talk to people about a topic or idea, and report back on that conversation in the next lesson. The task may specify whether the people should be young or old, or with particular experiences. The topic or idea may be described in a single word (such as 'revolution' or 'religion'), or a picture (such as a piece of art), or a piece of music or a television programme.

    The work may be set as homework that prepares pupils for the next piece of classwork (and it can kick-start an otherwise daunting topic), or that recapitulates work already completed. Conversations may be memorized, or shorter conversations might be transcribed word for word.

    Subject-specific examples of these kinds are given in the next few tasks. In all, the teacher setting the homework will be demonstrating how important the topic is, and how important it is that pupils talk about it to others. **(H7)**

◆ As part of the introduction to a **history** topic on 'revolutions', including the Industrial Revolution and the French Revolution, the pupils could be required to ask five adults what they understand by the word 'revolution'.

    The next lesson should start with a brainstorm of all the answers, to be used, for example, to categorize different types of revolution (e.g. social, political, technological), different qualities of revolutions (e.g. disruptive, exciting, progressive, violent), and different attitudes to revolutions (positive and negative). It may also allow for discussion of the complexity of concepts, different perspectives on history, and levels of understanding amongst adults.

Pupils can find such work very affirming, as they realize, at least after the lessons following this exercise, that they have a wider understanding of a concept than many adults. Adults can take pleasure in seeing young people learning so much, and in the value of homework itself. **(H9)**

◆ At almost any stage of an **RE** course, it might be valuable setting the homework task of talking to people much older or younger than themselves about key concepts in RE. The more general concepts (from the RE national guidance for pupils aged 11 to 14, from www.qca.org.uk) might include religion itself, or god, truth, life after death, authority, spirituality, ethics, forgiveness, evil, human rights, animal rights, social justice, citizenship or the environment.

Practising talking about these key concepts will also help with examination questions, and with questions asked by inspectors or interviewers. **(H15)**

◆ A picture like Picasso's *Guernica* can be used and studied in **art** and also in **citizenship** or **PSHE** or **English**. Pupils could be asked to talk to adults about the picture as a whole, or different groups of pupils might talk to adults about different elements of the picture. If adults can be found who have experienced war, their views would be most pertinent.

To record the conversations, the picture might be printed in the centre of a large sheet of paper, with speech bubbles around it, perhaps speech bubbles attached to characters in the picture, if the adults are to be asked what the characters might be thinking. Such homework will be seen to be engaging rather than punishing. **(H17)**

◆ Pupils talk about **music** all the time. Or, rather, young people when they are not being pupils talk about music all the time. The class might agree on a piece of music, such as a current hit, or the music to a popular advert, or the theme tune to a television programme, or a recording, perhaps made available as a sound file on a school intranet, copyright permitting.

Comparing reactions to the music of other young people, with the reactions of adults, is a good generic homework task. The basis of the conversations could be asking what six adjectives would best describe the music, or what real or fictional character might have this as a theme tune, and why. A pleasurable task, much better than more routine tasks or the punishments associated with homework-related misdemeanours. **(H19)**

◆ In the early days of television, it might have seemed as though television was killing off the art of conversation. Yet as television became a background to most people's everyday home life, people conversed around the television, with the television programmes themselves contributing to the conversations.

Supporting and capturing television-centred conversation gives homework a special role in learning. Any subject might use a relevant programme, with **PE** homework to discuss the ways of implementing rules in two televised sports, **design and technology** homework on the evaluation of products on car programmes, or **geography** homework on news coverage of a current environmental issue. Such homework may take up time, but does so imperceptibly, as time flies when you are engaged in an interesting task. **(H1)**

◆ Pupils can transcribe real conversations, as a way of studying the 'real' rules of language. They could (audio or video) tape an everyday conversation or an unscripted piece of talk on television, such as one of the confessional chat shows. Having been taught rules of transcription, preferably including marks for pauses but no added 'literary' punctuation, pupils could transcribe a couple of minutes of the conversation.

When done properly, this is a fascinating exercise, and can certainly provide material for many good follow-up lessons. Pupils are often most impressed, after this exercise, that actors manage to make scripted dialogue sound so natural, when scripts are so different to transcripts of conversations.

The exercise is also a good introduction in **English** to playwrights like Pinter or Beckett, who suddenly make more sense. Pupils may even realize how impressive it is that anyone understands the grammatically confused and apparently meaningless speech of everyday life. No more worrying over the 'right' answer. **(H5)**

◆ As a follow-up to the previous homework task, pupils could write a dialogue with all the characteristics of transcribed conversation. Tom Leonard wrote a beautifully ironic poem about 'thi six a clock news', saying 'if / a toktaboot / thi trooth / lik wanna yoo / scruff yi / widny thingk / it wuz troo'. The comedian Frankie Howerd had every 'ooh' and 'ah' scripted, and his apparently stuttering delivery was all obsessively rehearsed.

Scripting a realistic conversation, based on a style of talking used by people known to the pupils, is a tremendously difficult task, but one that, when successful, gives pupils a much improved sense of both written and spoken **English**. Pupils nearly always find scripting engaging. **(L7)**

◆ Pupils can also write imagined dialogues between other characters for **history**, **geography** or **citizenship**, such as an invader and a member of the indigenous population, or a defender and a critic of a cattle farmer in Brazil, or two politicians prior to an election.

Although realistic conversational scripts (with every pause and repetition included) is a challenge, more 'literary' scripts are often found easier by pupils. They are certainly found easier than most 'essay' styles. Combining dialogue-writing with topical, educationally relevant, debates, makes the homework even more important. **(H10)**

◆ Teaching is always a good way of learning, and pupils could be asked to teach a concept in any subject, or a phrase in **MFL**, to a member of their family, with the learner recording their achievement. This might be a regular homework task, set once a month in a number of subjects, though only if coordinated across subjects, to avoid education-overload in pupil homes.

Such involvement may seem an obvious technique, but it is done all too little in secondary schools: primary schools seem less inhibited. Parents will see homework as a positive, even useful, exercise, rather than as a form of punishment. **(H9)**

◆ For **MFL**, the family members might be interviewed (in English) about their childhood, as research for work on the perfect tense. With suitable preparation in class, including practising key phrases, pupils could write up these interviews in the target language. However, the real interest is generated by the initial questioning, which pupils will rarely find boring, as 'We are bored when we don't know what we are waiting for' (Benjamin 1999). **(L13)**

◆ Pupils could use family members as their interviewers, to help pupils prepare for mock job interviews in class. Pupils could prepare questions to be asked, as well as prepare for answering questions, in such interviews.

◆ Further research could also be carried out on a job or place of work of interest to the pupil, known to someone in the home or neighbourhood, properly exploiting people from outside the school. When pupils have completed such homework, the class can quickly build up a collection of materials to be kept in the careers library. **(L18)**

◆ Online chat is so important to young people today, that exploiting such chat has become a fine opportunity for effective homework. Pupils can be asked to discuss a news item in a lesson – perhaps a **PSHE** or **citizenship** lesson, and for homework to continue discussing the question on an online virtual learning environment (such as Blackboard, LearnLinc, Moodle, Sakai, Think.com). Pupils can be asked to do this regularly, every week, and will often get into the habit of participation, and will be able to see that other pupils are already involved in the virtual learning environment. Teachers are able to become 'unnecessary', as the discussions become part of the pupils' ordinary lives. **(L12)**

2. 'Hobby' homework

What hobbies do pupils have these days? According to Hallam (2004), the most common leisure (not hobby) activity of school pupils is watching television, followed by 'going out', playing with friends, taking part in sport, listening to music, reading, then playing with a computer. Watching television, going out, and playing with friends can hardly be called 'hobbies', but sport, music, reading and computers are clearly hobbyish activities.

It is a little strange that three of the subjects most closely associated with these hobbies have expressed problems with setting homework. **PE, music** and **ICT** teachers often say how difficult it is to set homework. For that reason alone, developing homework activities that capture some of those hobbies would be worthwhile. The increasing sophistication of Wii activities – including music and dance and sports – combines elements of all three subjects to be set for homework.

An even better reason for exploiting hobbies for homework is the commonly reported problem of homework tasks pushing hobbies aside, complained about by pupils and their parents since the 1920s at least. Would it not be better to recognize the interests of the pupils, as part of the school's approach to homework, rather than force pupils to make the choice?

Some of the following tasks exploit the hobbies and other leisure activities of pupils, others try to stimulate such activities. They might be set regularly and systematically for **PSHE** or **citizenship** homework, or occasionally for any subject, by expecting pupils to report on interests and hobbies, so that the school can understand what they do and what inspires them.

◆ The first hobby homework is about hobbies themselves, and is adapted from a **history** suggestion of Clare (1995). Pupils should put the following hobbies in order of preference, and explain why the best one is best: listening to music, going dancing, writing to friends (in any form, including texting), sport, reading, keeping a diary.

They should answer once for themselves, and once again for a person of the same age living in the historical period being studied, perhaps a young member of the royal household in the late fifteenth century, or someone growing up in Germany in the 1930s. Rather than taking time away from good things in life, this task, as so many hobby tasks, helps pupils to concentrate directly on those good things. **(H2)**

◆ Hobbies often generate favourite objects. Avid readers will have a favourite book, those into sport or music may have trophies, collectors will have whatever is collected. A number of subjects can exploit such special objects:

• an **English** homework task might be to write a persuasive piece explaining why the object should be saved from a fire;
• a **design and technology** homework task might be to analyse the design or manufacturing features that make the object special;
• an **RE** homework task might be to explore the symbolism and deep meaning of objects, related to work on sacred artefacts.

Resources from beyond the school are thereby recognized and valued. **(L17)**

◆ The various **technology** and **arts** subjects also themselves create objects, a picture, a song, a cake, that are good responses to the familiar question 'What did you do in school today?' These objects can themselves be favourite objects and can develop into hobbies. The more that can be completed as homework, either the manufacturing itself, the preparatory analysis or the subsequent evaluation, the more likely it is that the activity will turn into a hobby. **(L1)**

◆ It may be a stereotype of children, that they are the only people who can explain electronic equipment to adults, but a homework task asking them to do this, based on finding out exactly what the difficulties are, and perhaps writing up their advice in an instruction booklet, could be an interesting longer-term or holiday task, based on the real fondness of most teenagers for using electronic devices. Family members, helped by these guides, would be empowered by the pupils' **ICT** or **technology** homework. **(L5)**

◆ Pupils can be asked to bring in photographs (either their own, or postcards) or videos, related to specific hobbies or interests or activities. It might be for work on weddings and other celebrations or festivals, geographical features, or the design of buildings.

However 'real' are the illustrations in commercial teaching materials, pupils are likely to respond more to illustrations taken from the lives of their fellow pupils. Sensitivity is needed, of course, to avoid pupils being embarrassed, and the educational purpose of the work must be stressed, and families told about this, so that the activity will not be interpreted as simply being nosy.

For pupils or families who have difficulties with the activity, an alternative task can be set, such as a written description of events and places. The incentive for pupils to bring in their homework, though, is often considerable, when a trusting relationship has been created in the school. Such a relationship is always worth striving for by teachers and pupils alike. **(H12)**

◆ Shopping does not appear on many lists of hobbies for young people, perhaps because it is usually combined with other activities such as going out with friends. Yet shopping is not only important to young people, but vital to all families: vital in terms of culture and the meaning of life, and vital in terms of economic survival and status.

An **MFL** shopping homework task (adapted from one suggested in the TES of 29 May 2005) asks pupils to provide fashion advice for a celebrity (perhaps a celebrity in the school, perhaps the MFL teacher?), in the target language, based on specified online shopping sites in the target language.

Pupils tend to be keen to offer advice, even when it is not wanted, so they are liable to be even more keen when it *is* wanted: the deadline cannot come soon enough. **(L15)**

◆ A favourite **RE** shopping homework task asks pupils, studying the gifts given in the early years of Jesus' life, to describe some of the shops they will visit in the next few days.

Divide up shops between different pupils: one pupil or one group identified with newsagents, one with supermarkets, one with do-it-yourself stores, one with garden centres, one with convenience stores, one with fast-food outlets. Each pupil, or group of pupils, has to identify from their shop, the most appropriate gift for the newborn Jesus, and justify this gift.

Teachers who set this task have often been fascinated to hear what their pupils will suggest: the task seems to inspire particularly imaginative, entertaining and thoughtful responses. **(H16)**

◆ Listening to and performing music is one of the most popular of hobbies. It has already been suggested that talking about **music** is a helpful 'chat show' homework task. The hobbiness of music can be developed further.

Pupils can be asked to listen to six pieces of music, during a week, with the pieces to be listened to belonging to particular categories: two examples of 'chart' music, two examples of music used in advertising, two examples of music heard in a public place (such as a shop). The pupils might be asked to report back on these pieces, in terms of instrumentation, purpose, mood, effect on the listeners, or style. It may be better to stop the pupils from writing down their analyses for homework: remembering the pieces, and being able to describe and analyse them in class should help them to listen with that much more care.

Careful listening helps time fly. After a lesson of analysis and discussion, the following homework task might appropriately be to produce a written report on the issues raised by the exercise. **(H3)**

◆ Performing **music** can be harder to set as a homework task, as the number of pupils who say they have the hobby of 'performing music' is considerably smaller than the number of pupils who say they have the hobby of 'listening to music'. Yet the options for performance have been widened with changes in technology and changes in syllabuses that, between them, allow for and require much more performance than earlier generations of out-of-class, and out-of-tune, recorder playing and singing practice.

Using a computer to edit together sound clips, to create and play a suitable musical accompaniment to a horror movie, could be described as both composition and performance, for example. Performance tasks are only able to be set with good preparation and support inside and beyond the school. Such tasks cannot simply be set at the last minute, as the pupils leave the lesson. When they work, though, they are powerful contributions to the curriculum. **(H13)**

◆ The hobbiness of music can be used for homework tasks around adding lyrics to a piece of music or additional verses to songs (for **music, English, PSHE** and **RE** homework, depending on the topic), whether these tasks are written down and handed in, or rehearsed to be performed in class. In **MFL**, pupils might be composing lyrics in a foreign language, too.

Using the results of this homework for class, year group or whole-school assemblies or end-of-term productions, creates connections across the whole school. **(L20)**

◆ Ecological issues are popular with and motivate many pupils. On the basis of surveys and research work, pupils might produce an ecology journal as a collective homework task in **science** or **geography**, telling others of the issues they feel are important. A simple list of ecological priorities (what is most important to you, fair trade, carbon footprint, recycling or whatever?), completed by individual pupils for homework, and then debated as a class follow-up, can engage pupils and allow for different worldviews to be acknowledged and aired. This would therefore provide an ideal opportunity to differentiate tasks according to the abilities and interests of pupils. Teachers can find such work an encouragement that their teaching has real implications for the next generation. **(L6)**

◆ Related work, well practised in primary schools, is to collect material for and build a bird's nest. The **design** implications, as well as the biology and environmental implications, are considerable. Indeed, the implications of admitting the creative skills of non-human animals is itself able to make the task worthwhile. **(L9)**

◆ Pupils' hobbies are, by their nature, voluntary, but if there is a responsible adult involved in the hobby, then the pupil, the pupil's family, and the teacher could work together to ask the adult to write a 'report' on how the pupil is doing.

Teachers often find it difficult wringing information about hobbies out of their pupils, so any such reports will be welcomed. Allowing reports on such hobbies to count as permission to miss some other homework in a related subject, might add to their value. However, as pupils are likely to be most keen on the subjects that complement their own hobbies, it may be better simply to see such reports as adding to the quality of the pupils' learning, providing encouragement from outside as well as inside the school. **(L19)**

◆ It is important not to leave out pupils who have responsibilities outside school that go far beyond 'hobbies'. Some pupils work long hours doing paid work on weekdays or weekends, or doing housework or caring for other members of their families. As with hobbies, information about such work rarely gets to teachers, and yet it can be of enormous value to pupils' education.

Paid work often brings out the responsible and mature quality of pupils. Housework and caring may be done skilfully and sensitively. Looking after younger brothers and sisters may be relevant to **PE**, **design and technology** or **English**, depending on what is done. Shop work may benefit **maths** or **ICT**, too.

Such achievements are valuable in themselves, and pupils deserve to be credited with them when it comes to assessment. Teachers should welcome reports from work supervisors or parents or those cared for, and could add these to reports and other records of achievement. Reporting of this kind will also be encouraged if regular homework tasks require a signature from a recipient; for example, asking pupils to make a meal at home, with 'report cards' to be filled in by those who eat the food. **(L16)**

3. 'Inclusion' homework

The word 'inclusion' seems to be everywhere these days, and 'inclusive schooling' has taken over from predecessors such as 'community schooling' and 'comprehensive schooling', as the term roughly meaning 'local schooling for local people'. Inclusion also addresses issues:

◆ special needs, inclusion meaning pupils being taught alongside each other, and pupils actively working together;

◆ racism and sexism in the curriculum and throughout the school;

◆ family involvement, often also addressing issues of social class; and

◆ health, with 'healthy schooling' another alternative to describe 'local schooling for local people'.

As far as this section of the book goes, 'inclusion' homework tasks try to capture something of the communal life of pupils beyond the classroom. It is therefore close to the other 'capture' homework activities, especially the 'chat show' ones. What can be added to them is the idea of bringing people together in ways that help make the school that much more inclusive.

Continuing the theme of personal connection, it is possible, for homework, to tap into the real worlds and beliefs of the world beyond the classroom. Back in the 1980s, Jeffcoate demonstrated that 4-year-old pupils, shown pictures of people with a range of ethnicities, demonstrated no racism when talking to teachers, but demonstrated considerable racism (captured by hidden microphones) when talking to their peers (reported in Carrington and Troyna 1988).

This degree of understanding, by 4-year-olds, of when it is more or less 'appropriate' to appear racist, astonished many teachers. Yet there are other ways in which pupils can be wildly different with teachers than they are with peers and family. Mostly, it is not that pupils are 'better' or 'worse' in one place or another: they are just different. Garrulous in class, quiet at home, or the other way around, sociable or anti-social, a responsible carer or irresponsibly self-centred, thoughtful or thoughtless. These contrasts are the stuff of parents' evenings.

In the build-up to parents' evenings, there is usually a report written on every pupil. In the build-up to report-writing, there is usually the homework diary. Homework diaries are the most common way of teachers and pupils' families swapping information about homework. Teachers who take the diaries seriously will be able to develop the homework and the inclusion of families, through these diaries. Writing brief explanatory notes (such as 'No English homework is mentioned, because it was all set at the start of term') may be helpful; reading and responding to any notes from parents will be essential.

If the pupils go home and parents do not see any homework in the diary, the parents may worry about the children ('did you forget to write the homework in your diary?') or worry about the teachers ('did they not set you any homework?'). In both cases, they may write a note in the diary complaining about homework. Teachers need to respond with care, and only after discussing the situation with the pupil. This correspondence therefore fits neatly into report-writing and parents' evenings, which themselves should always include helpful ideas on how homework might further support learning in a subject.

Reports often simply describe the absence or presence of home-work, rather than its effect on learning. The latter will prove more helpful to pupils and to their families, and will also prove more inclusive.

Homework can try to explore and exploit more sides of pupils than they normally show to any one group, and the list of 'inclusion' homework tasks starts with an activity that can bring together not only a class, but a year group, the school as a whole, the local com-munities, and people through history. Not only that, it is a *maths* homework task.

Numbers are interesting in themselves, and maths should help pupils understand number: surprisingly difficult with large numbers. This task can be set for **maths**, and also **history**, **RE** and **PSHE** homework and classwork, and developed in class or year group or whole-school assemblies. It was originally developed to help children understand the number 6,000,000, a number referred to in lessons on the Shoah (the holocaust of the 1930s–1940s):

◆ In class, pupils are given a sheet covered in 10,000 dots.

Starting towards the end of the lesson, to be completed for homework, individual pupils, or if possible groups of two or three friends, should label each dot with the name of a person they know, personally, who is not a member of that class. They can label with initials and arrows, and should start with the top left-hand corner of the page of dots, labelling dots close together. The people named may be friends or family or neighbours, past and present, as long as they are personally known to the pupils: celebrities do not count.

Handing the homework in, the sheets can be displayed: few pupils will have been able to label more than 100 dots (and it is not a competition, in any case).

The teacher should then get the pupils to help roll out five rolls of paper, each roll consisting of 20 sheets of A3 paper with each sheet having six times 10,000 dots on it. (These dimensions have been carefully practised in many school settings.) The 'roll out' (in a large classroom, or better still in a corridor or hall) will reveal exactly six million dots. This must only be done after the homework task of labelling: the pupils will understand large numbers, and will understand 6,000,000, in a way that they did not before. So will teachers.

It may seem like a simple set of class and homework tasks, but it has given many pupils and teachers sleepless nights. They are upset at the thought of the large number, whether it is applied to the Shoah, deaths in other wars, or as the result of poverty. Large numbers are worth knowing, personally; people are worth knowing, in large numbers. **(L18)** The following pages show what ten thousand dots look like.

....
....
....
....
....
....
....
....
....
....
....

....
....
....
....
....
....
....
....
....
....

....
....
....
....
....
....
....
....
....
....

....
....
....
....
....
....
....
....
....
....

....
....
....
....
....
....
....
....
....
....

◆ Continuing the theme of personal connection, homework can recognize some of the different realities of pupils with their peers and families, as well as the side of themselves they choose to present in classrooms. Some teachers say 'Parents equal trouble', when it comes to **religion, citizenship**, or controversial topics in **history**. They may even say that the teacher's job is to 'get pupils to forget the prejudices of their families', or 'Migration is too sensitive an issue in this area, so we will only study migration in the USA'.

Yet family views do not go away if we ignore them: pupils simply learn two ways of thinking about the world, one way for school, another for home. And rejecting parents usually rebounds on teachers. Parents, and now even governments, become just as likely to say that 'teachers equal trouble' or 'Our job is to get children to forget the prejudices of their teachers'. On migration, then, as an example, pupils can be set the homework of asking peers and adults questions about the topic:

- Interview three people who have not lived in the same place all their lives, one who has moved within this country, and two who have moved between countries (including countries within the UK).
- Describe in detail their reasons for moving or migration, as well as their movements. If the responses are appropriately anonymized, they could be combined, as an extremely useful and 'real' view of reasons for moving.

A simpler task would be to ask pupils to write about why they have lived where they have lived, with reasons being given for staying in one place, as much as for moving. This can be annotated on to a Google Maps (from www.google.co.uk) or Multimap (www.multimap.com) map. Teachers can demonstrate how much they value pupils' personal knowledge of migration. **(H7)**

◆ Other real questions that can be asked of real people, might be asked of people who have lived through different significant periods or events. Older people are likely to have more to talk about in such interviews, but young people live through important events, too, and pupils can interview fellow pupils about these events. Realizing that the past is now, as well as 'a long time ago', is a lesson in itself. A sensitive and important topic (of the **PSHE** and **RE** curriculum as well as of life) is death.

- Pupils might think about their own lives and write their own obituary, imagining they lived to be 100 (and perhaps making use of a paper or online newspaper obituary section, or online memorial website such as catless.ncl.ac.uk/VMG/), and they could ask peers and adults about what they think happens after they die.
- They might practise writing a letter to a bereaved friend, or complete some creative writing having looked at some poetry on the topic.

It goes without saying that such work is to be handled sensitively: most school-leavers will have lost (through death) a close member of their family, and most will at some time have contemplated killing themselves. Talking to people about the issues is not an alternative to ignoring the issues. Talking to people is an alternative to worrying about it on your own. **(L2)**

◆ Still looking at some of the sadder issues in society, when a large employer closes down, many people are affected beyond the employees who lose their jobs. A touching **geography** homework task involves a 'talking head' activity. Pupils draw a picture of someone their age (and this may be a self-portrait), and draw and fill in a speech bubble, explaining how that person feels about the closure of the local employer. (The employer might be chosen for its relevance to the area in which the pupils live.) Pupils will often write very sensitively about the personal and family implications, and teachers can in this way 'admit' into the classroom some of the concerns of pupils and their families. **(L9)**

◆ On a cheerier note, pupils can come together, in homework, to complete group work in **history**.

- A class studying the French Revolution might be divided, and asked for homework to research either the Monarch, the First Estate, the Second Estate or the Third Estate.
- The homework could be to find information, or to use the information gathered in class to speculate on what their group's lives would have been like at the start of the revolution.
- In the next lesson, the class would be re-arranged into groups of four, with one Monarch and one member of each Estate in

each group. They would then have to use the information discovered or learnt for homework to write a short scene or role-play about a meeting between these four people in Paris in 1789.

A similar task could be set up, with pupils preparing for a role play about a tribunal hearing during the First World War. (Perhaps this is not so cheery, after all.) Once pupils are used to this approach to group work, their motivation to complete the work is considerable, so that their groups are not let down. **(L15)**

◆ In recent years, many lessons have been given on lotteries, to exploit pupils' interest. There is something uncomfortable about teachers seeming to promote a lottery for which pupils are mostly too young to buy tickets. Yet there are many opportunities for good work on probability that will 'include' the beliefs and lives of people outside school, including some common **mathematical** misunderstandings.

How do people choose their numbers, and are choices based on beliefs that certain numbers, or combinations of numbers, are more or less likely to be chosen, or on 'lucky number' beliefs? Either way, there is work to be done on probabilities. Who would be prepared to buy a ticket every week with the same numbers as the previous week's winning numbers, or with six consecutive numbers?

Pupils can do useful survey work on such issues, with much follow-up work on the results of the surveys as well as their own beliefs about the lottery. The association of such tasks with winning money, itself makes them more attractive to pupils. **(H19)**

◆ Homes may not always be equipped for practical work, but all homes are packed with the products of artists, musicians and designers. Many of these products are unrecognized, ironically, precisely because they are popular. A small number of houses are described as 'architect-designed', as though other houses just came together by chance. In fact, 'architect-designed' refers to the status, pay and qualifications of the person designing the house, not the fact that it was designed in contrast to randomly constructed houses.

Homework in **design and technology** can help pupils to see all objects as designed, and therefore to become more aware of the designedness of their environments. If pupils are discussing with their families or friends the buildings in the street, and the objects in their homes, they are completing real homework: work on their distinctive, individual, *homes*. **(L14)**

◆ For many years, people have tended to think of artists, musicians and designers as individual creative spirits, and products as easily attributable to such single geniuses. This belies the co-operative creativity of past times and other cultures, such as the emergence and development of folk songs, vernacular architecture or decorative sculptures on medieval cathedrals. It also belies the cooperative nature of much of what is thought of as 'solo' creativity, with debates over the contributions of uncredited painters in ceramic workshops of 'names' like Clarice Cliff, or the influence of producers and session musicians on 'stars' like Lennon and McCartney.

The cooperative creativity demonstrated here is not a problem (unless you are the person being accused of being less of a genius), but an opportunity, a potential strength, and it can play a big role in the way in which **art**, **music** and **design and technology** are taught, and how homework can be set. Looking for cooperation can mean creating a sense of collaborative and communal endeavour, critical for a school's own inclusiveness.

For example, a car will have been developed by a team including specialists in manufacturing, in electrical systems, in design aesthetics, in aerodynamics, in economics, in marketing, and many more processes; a house will have been developed by a team including specialists in surveying, in materials, in architecture, in marketing, and many more processes. The teacher should choose one type of object, and work with the pupils in class to analyse the different people involved in developing that object. For homework, the pupils should be put into groups and given each of these roles, with the task being to come up with a cooperatively produced design for a product. **(L20)**

◆ Including pupils themselves, and their families, is a role often given to **art**, **RE** and **English**. These subjects are all significant for developing pupils' self-image, and investigating stereotypes, just as they develop technical skills, knowledge and aesthetic-moral values.

Pupils learn to look at themselves and others around them, to observe their home and school, and the environment beyond.

The subjects can be routes into cultures that are otherwise impenetrable, and can link otherwise diverse traditions and cultures. A simple task such as sketching a member of the household, or doing a close observation study of the front door, can help a pupil understand both the object of the study, its significance and meaning, and the methods of capturing it.

A similarly simple task, originally set for art but equally useful for English and RE, is to collect the signatures of six adults, and write an account of what can be learnt from the signatures. Pupils find it enormously enjoyable discovering the 'secrets' revealed by artwork or handwriting. **(L11)**

◆ More personal self-development, in a way that can create more inclusion, would be provided by **PSHE** homework based around assertiveness training.

- Pupils could practise saying 'No' in a confident voice, making it clear to bullies that they are not going to react in a passive, child-like, way (for example by bursting into tears or pleading for mercy) or in an aggressive way. They could practise this technique on members of their own family, if possible as a role-play.
- Pupils could also practise other assertiveness techniques such as the 'broken record' technique and 'fogging'. The broken record technique (for those brought up on digital recordings) means repeating a short phrase, as would happen with a broken record.

The phrase might be 'I'm not going to give you my money', 'Why don't we talk about this', or perhaps simply 'No', and should be repeated until the bully is tired of saying whatever bullies might say.

It is a surprisingly good way to deal with other people's aggression. The words in the repeated phrase may eventually get through to the aggressor's mind, as long as the repeated phrase itself is not aggressive and contains no 'trigger' words (so 'Let's just sit down' is better for repeating than 'Put the *knife* down').

- 'Fogging' is a special kind of response to bullying. This 'accepts' an insult, and renders it insignificant. If someone says 'Fatty', aggressively, to a heavy person, then the recipient could say 'You are right, I am heavy' or 'Yes, and I've heard that before: can you think of something more original?'

Pupils practising responses to bullies and other insulters, for homework, can build up a good sense of assertiveness all round the class, and the homework is enjoyed as a game in itself. **(H5)**

◆ Pupils, despite themselves, look at newborn or very young babies with a sense of awe undoubtedly sufficient to stimulate good **art** and **English** and **science** and **RE** work. Inequality of access to babies, makes setting this work for homework challenging, but the classwork used to stimulate homework could be a visit from a teacher on maternity leave, or from a parent or sibling of a pupil with a young baby.

Videos of newborn babies could help, but the real thing is always preferable, if only for stimulating more senses and emotions, and therefore being that much more memorable. **(L4)**

◆ Whatever topic has been taught, a homework task that can be set near the end of the topic, prior to a final piece of assessment, is to ask pupils to create a study guide for future pupils studying the same topic. Such guides, written by and for pupils, can sometimes be, embarrassingly, better than guides produced by teachers. They are sure to be helpful in bringing together pupils of different ages, over time: the educational value of the task is clear to all. **(H10)**

◆ Right at the end of a topic, pupils can be set a homework in which they give a list of questions to other members of their families. The list of questions, either set by the teacher or, better, set by the pupils, are 'Ask me' questions (described in Lawrence-Lightfoot 2003: 64). For example, 'Ask me what is really interesting about Buddhism' in **RE**, or 'Ask me why friction is so important' in **science**. Reporting back on the homework will involve pupils describing how the conversation developed, rather than a written submission. Homework can in this way inspire encouragement from beyond the school. **(L19)**

Capturing the world of pupils, drawing people together in conversations and in creative activity, this chapter helps build up trust between all the members of the school and local community. It also helps make the curriculum that much richer and more meaningful to pupils. The book is getting closer to preventing the abolition of homework, but before it does that, abolition should be tackled head-on. That is the topic of the next chapter.

4 | Homework that dares not speak its name

Homework in this chapter

Geography	95, 97, 99–100
History	96, 97, 98, 100–1
Maths	96
MFL	98
RE	97–8, 101
Science	95, 97

Let's call the whole thing off!

By the time a book gets to Chapter 4, it can be assumed that readers (if not those who merely flick) will have some kind of commitment. Yet even the greatest fans of homework will at times hate it enough to want to kill it off altogether. I have been involved in homework policy for 17 years, and every few months throughout that time, someone has been in the paper suggesting killing off homework – most recently, as a result of a piece of research by the Association of Teachers and Lecturers (Milne 2008b). Chapter 4 will try to satisfy the wish to kill homework, and will see what happens. Killing off homework has some interesting consequences. Some abolish homework, and reinvent it under another name. Others try to get rid of the home from homework, and survive the amputation. Still more merrily, why not send the pupils off on holiday, and swap the dour evenings by the kitchen table for happier days by the sea? In all these ways, teachers are overcoming a whole range of administrative and organizational problems raised by homework, and ticking off the hate-codes as they go.

1. 'Abolition' homework

Teachers would be appalled if a large group of pupils missed a day a week of school, or if they missed all the lessons in two of their subjects, for several years. Yet teachers are rarely surprised if they hear that a pupil has done no homework for years, or a class has been set no homework for years, which is a similar loss of up to 20 per cent of their education.

Some teachers say that there is no point setting homework for certain pupils, because they simply would not or could not do it. It would be more trouble than it was worth, it would cause too much trouble, even to ask. This is not entirely unreasonable, especially in a chapter on abolishing homework. It only becomes unfair or unreasonable if it is applied to some pupils or classes, while other pupils or classes are expected to do large amounts of homework. If a large number of pupils can do no homework, this is a good reason for total abolition. That would at least provide equal, if fewer, opportunities for all.

If homework were abolished:

◆ Pupils might have more equal opportunities, as all their work would be done in school, under similar conditions, with fewer advantages given to those pupils with desks and encyclopaedias at home.

◆ A department or a school that set no homework might have more tightly organized lessons, as teachers could no longer say 'Finish this at home', and pupils might have less stress, not worrying all evening about homework they should be doing.

However:

◆ Such a school would either be under pressure to extend its day or cut back on its staff.

◆ The abolition of homework would mean either less work being completed by pupils (because other schools have homework to extend learning time), or a wasteful use of teaching staff (because other schools use homework to extend learning time without extending teaching time).

◆ To recover that time, rather than extending the school day by adding lessons, the school might instead have extra sessions of relatively independent study, during which pupils would do what would otherwise have been set as homework. Of course, this has already been done: many boarding schools have 'prep' instead of homework, with an hour or two of supervised private study at the end of lessons.

If we abolished homework, then, we might simply reinvent it, as suggested in a newspaper article, 'Down with homework – bring back prep!' (quoted in MacBeath and Turner 1990).

Suppose that every school decided to abolish homework, as has happened in several countries. Would that provide more equal opportunities, and a less stressful life for pupils? Perhaps, but talking to teachers in countries with little or no formal homework provides evidence that abolishing homework is something of an illusion. Homes and families help their children with their work, whether or not formal homework is set. Some homes and families help more than others, and issues of equal opportunities again arise.

Abolishing homework ends up being as inequitable as abolishing compulsory education. Education itself would not be abolished, just the educational opportunities of a large portion of the population. Equal opportunities may require some homework, then, simply to formalize and make more equitable the help that can be given to pupils outside school. Here, then, are some abolitionist homework tasks.

◆ The most common 'abolition' homework is the project, as described in Lee (2005) (quoted in the next chapter). Many departments set a big project as a 'non-homework', lasting anything up to a term. The planning and development of the project is the responsibility of the pupils, who are often reported as enjoying the work all the more, as it is so much their own. Careful guidance on project topics is needed, notably for those pupils who have had difficulty succeeding in school learning. Those are the very pupils likely to benefit most from such a structure.

Such investigative work is central to **history**, **geography**, **science**, **design and technology**, **English**, **art**, **citizenship**: almost all subjects, in the end. Extended projects, for 'non-homework', can therefore play a vital strategic role in the curriculum. They are alternatives to the all-too-common hurriedly set, disjointed and purposeless, homework tasks set at the end of many lessons. **(H13)**

◆ Another form of abolition homework is to have a policy that there can be no *written* homework. This abolishes a kind of homework, but retains the possibility of all the 'chat show' and many other homework tasks that ask pupils to talk, listen, watch or think. Those skills need developing, so the abolition of written homework may achieve an improvement in the all-round development of pupils.

Listening to even the blandest of chart music, for example, might require spotting sources of musical styles. Chart music in recent years has influences from way beyond its folk and blues roots: the influences of the Americas, Africa, South Asia and many parts of Europe can all be heard.

Pupils coached to listen, for homework, will be much better prepared for the comparatively straightforward 'spotting' exercises used for example in some GCSE **music** exams. Teachers may enjoy 'marking' such homework, as it involves listening in class rather than taking a pile of books home. **(H14)**

◆ Not setting reading, but having books available to be read, is a form of voluntary almost-homework that affects many pupils. Having almost any books around the school and around the home is likely to help children, without the books ever being forced on children. Mary Stuart in Sussex has worked with university students who were the first in their families to go to university. One of the most important differences between those 'first generation' students who succeeded, and those who dropped out, was the number of books available in their homes when growing up.

It is not that schools should feel responsible for giving books to families, but it is reasonable to ask that teachers give recommendations of books that might be helpful for families, as presents or prizes, and perhaps even arrange to have book stalls at parents' evenings.

And those teachers worried about the 'quality' of the books available at home, should be comforted by the knowledge that people can read books in many different ways. Children may read 'rubbish' and they may know how bad the book is, and enjoy making fun of it, just like adults often enjoy watching and criticizing television programmes they think are 'rubbish'. The role of the teacher is to give pupils those critical tools and the enthusiasm for critique to go with them.

Homework tasks are not separated from the development of critical skills in classwork: they are the result, at home, of what goes on in class. High status non-homework means that teachers associate homework with learning, not with punishments. **(H16)**

◆ Residential school trips include trips abroad, adventure or sporting activities, musical or drama tours. All require teachers to worry 24-hours-a-day, and all require pupils to learn 24-hours-a-day. For teachers, such trips combine the characteristics of teaching and parenting: sometimes positively (building up good relationships that will affect later classwork, as teachers are seen as more human, and pupils are seen as more responsible), sometimes negatively (as teachers try to deal with what would otherwise be parenting problems of late nights and other adolescent misbehaviours).

There is rarely a formal division, on such trips, between lessons and homework and leisure time. Homework is abolished and yet takes place throughout the trip. Learning is going on all the time, over meals, in the evenings. The learning can range across **personal and social skills**, **MFL** (if in a suitable country), **citizenship**, **RE**, **geography**, **music**, and so many other subjects.

Imaginative teachers may also use the ideas from residential trips to create 'non-homework' tasks without travelling: creating a virtual trip (a simulated trip, with visits to shops and places of interest, all online), or creating a French café at a parents' evening, staffed by pupils. Home and school come together in creative ways. **(H6)**

◆ For **PSHE** and **PE**, it is especially clear that abolishing homework would not abolish home work. In other words, nothing the school does could stop pupils developing, personally and physically, whilst out of school. Yet young people appear to be less fit than they were, and personal difficulties are all too common, and this probably has more to do with their lives outside school than the time or energy spent on school sports and lessons in PSHE.

Promoting physical and personal development outside school is therefore enormously important, whether or not it is officially called 'homework'.

- Walking to school, or sitting with good posture, or playing active games, or carrying shopping, or decorating a bedroom, or washing the car, can all be, and count as, PE homework, if they help pupils improve their skills, strength and endurance.
- A regular 'exercise audit' can be set as homework, listing and recording physical activities done. As with other homework audits, pupils who are dishonest may become more open if they are told how ineffective their apparent hard work is, given their current level of achievement in school.
- Games are part of PE and many PSHE syllabuses, and are part of pupils' lives outside school. Surveying and describing games, including the games of younger sisters and brothers, games played in a local park, or the range of computer games, can help pupils understand their variety.
- There are many variations on more standard games, and describing the 'alternative rules' of such games can be a challenging task for pupils.

Teachers will find their work has an effect beyond lessons, if the non-homework is well set. **(L8)**

◆ Pupils may, in the build-up to exams, recommend exercise to each other, as a way of solving the boredom and stress of revision. Revision can be completed whilst on an exercise bike, and memory games can be played while running or swimming. As homework, this would have the magical property of combining two homework tasks in the time it takes to do either one of them. (The same might be said of completing homework whilst the television is on, or in a kitchen while people are preparing food.)

Revision is rarely thought of in the same way as ordinary homework, so this is a double-abolition as well as a double homework. Round-the-house chess is a variation on the same theme, and was invented by computer pioneers Alan Turing and David Champernowne in the 1940s. A player makes a move in a chess match, runs around the house (or to the end of the street and back, or to the ground floor and back), and if this is completed before the opponent has moved, makes another move.

The game could be adapted to use any other board game, and, with a bit of thought, to computer games too. Older pupils might adapt it as a revision exercise, setting each other tasks: 'Name ten parts of a cell', 'Write down six important causes of World War One'. Time is not saved, but doubled. **(H1)**

◆ Other study skills and revision homework, that may not be thought of as homework, includes listing the minutes or hours spent on homework (as also mentioned in Chapter 5), producing revision plans, or listing resources needed. Sometimes, with really stressed pupils, it may be helpful to avoid revision timetables, and plan, instead, a leisure timetable: a list of all the times in the week when the pupil can eat, sleep, and have fun. Then, the pupil can fill in the rest of the time with studying. A strange idea, maybe, but it works by making pupils feel less guilty about having a rest, and more rested when it comes to study times.

Promoting relaxation when not working is all too rarely done. Being idle means getting nothing done, and this is a bad thing. Being lazy means enjoying doing nothing, or enjoying relaxing, and this is a good thing. Secondary school homework is usually recommended as lasting between 4 and 15 hours a week, depending on the age of the child. Even at the busiest times, pupils should have plenty of time to relax or to do completely 'non-school' things. Instead, many pupils spend several years constantly worrying about work they should be doing, but not doing it or leaving it to the last minute.

There is a considerable difference between five hours' worrying plus one hour's work, and one hour's work plus five hours' relaxing: the former is the punishment of the idle, the latter is the luxury of the lazy. It is this difference that makes classwork (started early in the day) less worrisome than homework (often started late in the evening). **(H18)**

This 'abolition' section is completed by noting that abolishing homework is not the same as putting it off or organizing it badly: putting something unpleasant off is likely to create worry and stress, abolishing something unpleasant is likely to create relief and happiness.

Some teachers, therefore, need to be told that saying 'There is no homework this week: we will catch up next week', is not abolition and can cause unnecessary stress. And, as Hargreaves says, 'A poor homework policy and/or practice makes its contribution to enlarging the achievement gap between advantaged and disadvantaged pupils'.

2. 'Homeless' homework

A small number of pupils are, literally, homeless. Many more have homes that are not well suited to completing many homework tasks, either because of the facilities available, the number of people competing for facilities, or the number of responsibilities the pupil has such as caring for others.

Guides to homework often suggest that families can best help by providing a quiet room, a desk and study equipment such as a computer, although worries about unchecked computer access have led to more recommendations of keeping children's computers in 'public' areas of the house. Quiet 'work station' facilities may still indeed be useful, even if most pupils claim they work better with the noise of music, television or conversation around them. Yet it is also important for teachers to plan homework tasks that do not require any such facilities, as there will always be some pupils without them.

◆ All the tasks that can be completed in school can be regarded as 'homeless' homework. Schools can support this work by how the school and the school day are organized.

- Allowing pupils to come early to school, if supported by breakfast clubs, and allowing pupils to stay late, especially if supported by homework clubs (described in Chapter 5, below), can help. There may well be transport issues in rural schools where most pupils are bussed to and from school.
- Lunchtimes may allow for more homework if they are longer, and if pupils are allowed to work in a number of quiet areas such as empty classrooms.

Providing such study areas alongside other clubs, is a more positive response to the problems caused by lunchtime mis-behaviour, than the response involving cutting down lunch hours to half-hours.

Break-times and even brief breaks between lessons may provide further support for in-school homework, if pupils are allowed to stay inside. There is no question that all these sug-gestions have staffing and management implications. They are presented, knowing this, as ways of supporting more equitable homework, and the costs for a school to provide more facilities are likely to be much lower than the costs to provide the equiva-lent facilities in all the pupils' homes.

The kinds of homework task best suited to such work include homework that supports school-based performance, such as preparing for a year-group or whole-school assembly perform-ance. **(L10)**

◆ Helpful in-school support can be provided by the school library and computer resources. It is critical that teachers understand how the library and other learning resources are used, and how available they are outside lesson times.

- Are there any special revision sessions or access rights in the holidays or on evenings or at weekends before important exams?
- Are public libraries also recommended, and when are they available?
- Are particular reference books such as dictionaries recom-mended?

Schools may provide book stalls or course guides or special events for all concerned with the school, linked to such facilities, and all would help provide a good home for otherwise homeless homework. A good strategy used by some teachers and librarians is to get groups of pupils to choose a certain number of books or other resources to be added to the library on a particular subject.

In this way, the pupils may feel more like the library is 'theirs', even if the resources are the same as would have been chosen by teachers or librarians working on their own.

This also illustrates the value of teaching and library staff training and working closely together, to promote independent learning skills in homework. They will also avoid the frustrating problem that all too many library staff come across: 150 pupils coming to them in the same week, all having been set the same homework task 'Go to the library and find out about the Battle of Hastings'. Organizing homework better than that, teachers can gain tremendous support from the school-beyond-the-classroom. **(H11)**

◆ Schools are increasingly providing online support for classwork and homework. This has not happened quite as quickly as some had predicted. The vast majority of school websites have general information about the school and the work of pupils and staff, without the detailed curriculum plans and weekly homework tasks that could be there.

Setting up closed sites, available from any online computer, and accessible to pupils, school staff, and perhaps external learning mentors (for example from a local university), is now inexpensive and technically straightforward. Such virtual learning environments (or VLEs) are common in further and higher education. Local authorities are increasingly using VLEs to help provide specialist support for pupils unable to come to school, or spread over a large area studying unusual exam subjects.

Commercially or freely available VLEs include Think.com (www.think.com/), Blackboard (www.blackboard.com), Sakai (sakaiproject.org/), Moodle (moodle.org) and LearnLinc (www.learnlinc.com/). All can host and support homework and other forms of independent learning. All can provide opportunities for setting and supporting homework for those pupils without good home facilities, but only if pupils have good computing facilities available in school, after-school clubs, local libraries, community centres, and the often under-recognized resources in the homes of friends and relatives.

Homework set in this form is often characteristically 'aboli-tion' homework. There may be VLE-supported mentoring systems available in a number of schools and local authorities, and these can be relatively easily set up, perhaps working along-side teacher training organizations. Working on VLEs can break down geographical boundaries, and can certainly make 'handing in homework' easier than carrying a heavy bag of books to and from school: a back-breaking problem highlighted by Kralovec and Buell (2000). **(H12)**

◆ Those teachers who feel that homework is more about homes being involved in celebrating what pupils do, may have fond memories of very young pupils taking paintings home to be magnetically attached to fridges. Few homes have fridges suit-able for displaying secondary-age schoolwork: even the largest fridges would be hard put to carry half a dozen pieces of GCSE coursework. Homeless fridge galleries may therefore be created online.

A blog (short for a web log, see www.blogger.com/ and www.bloggingbrits.co.uk/), is commonly used as a kind of diary of everyday life. It can be adapted to become a class- or subject-based blog. This could support memorable home–school links, and can do so without needing all the homes to have facilities for completing more traditional homework tasks. **(L5)**

◆ It is a cliché that a house is not a home: what makes something a home is the nature of the bonds between the people living there. Engagement with homes and neighbourhoods is a way of making homework necessary, and a way of creating homes (not houses) even when there seem to be none.

Group work in **art** might be completed by pupils on 'our homes', and later on 'our school', with each pupil contributing to a large display. The simplest technique would be to sketch at home, with final versions produced in class, but more complex work might, for example, mean creating ideal homes from char-acteristics of all the homes studied. Ideal, that is, as homes, not as houses.

The composite photography suggested in Chapter 3, above, could be expanded here, with a digitally stitched composite display on the theme of home-and-school. This could be con-structed in the form of expanding circles, at the centre of which could be those elements of most importance:

- pictures of pets, usually in the inner circle of significance, for anyone with a pet,
- a favourite seat, popular with Homer Simpson,
- a picture of a houseplant or garden plant grown by a pupil.

In the outer rings, would be elements of some significance, and the further out, the less significance. Teachers as well as pupils are generally entranced by these expanding circles of significance. **(L6)**

◆ The truly homeless may sleep under the stars, and this reminds us that homework might appropriately be as simple as looking at the sky at night. As Oscar Wilde reminded us, though we may all be lying in the gutter, at least some of us are looking at the stars.

Science and **art** work can be completed on the nature and meanings of stars and constellations. Light pollution in cities, and fears about children being out late at night, conspire to reduce opportunities for star-gazing, yet there must still be viable ways to recommend this. A nicely complementary task would be to have a view of the earth from space. This is easily available in satellite pictures from the Met Office (www. meto.gov.uk/) or Google Earth (earth.google.com), and, for any pupils travelling by air during holidays, from the window of an aircraft. Google Earth can itself be a way of finding a home in the world – a home near historical venues (for **history**), near sacred places (for **RE**), or near rainforests (for **geography**).

Again, art work or creative writing can result, as can detailed geographical work. Staring at the stars, or at the earth, can capture pupils for hours, and change their views of the world for years to come. **(L7)**

◆ Pupils in the later years of school may be planning to live on their own. Designing a bed-sit, including its furnishings, includes many separate tasks for individuals or small groups of pupils. Planning the **economics** of living in this way is even more complex, and even more useful. Lists of possible items can be produced, including daily and weekly items such as food, as well as longer-term items such as television licences and mobile and utility bills.

The conversations that follow, when pupils are tasked for homework to discuss what everything costs in their own homes, can be amongst the best **PSHE** education the pupils will receive, and all without a teacher in sight. **(L12)**

3. 'Holiday' homework

Some may say it is the ultimate in intrusion: to try to spoil holidays with homework. On the other hand, pupils say that holiday times combine presents and activities that are novel (that therefore involve learning) and periods of intense boredom (that might be relieved by some ideas from school). If school can exploit holidays for educational purposes, and can make holidays that much more enjoyable, then the trick will have been achieved of getting non-classwork completed without it appearing to be 'homework'.

Exploiting holidays for educational purposes is most important for those who take holidays during term time. Whether such holidays should be 'authorized' by the school, might reasonably be determined by whether the pupil is willing to complete educational activities whilst on holiday, to be reported back after the holiday. Schools can have ready-made holiday tasks, across every subject, for instant use if the occasion arises. Plans for more regular, and acceptable, holiday periods can be built in to curriculum planning, in various imaginative ways.

◆ A conventional homework task that could help create holiday homework, would invite pupils to produce, between them, a booklet of holiday advice relevant to the curriculum. This might be from the perspective of a single subject, focusing, say, on **geographical** advice, **scientific** advice or **literary** advice. It might include guidance on travelling-away holidays or stay-at-home holidays.

Prior to the summer holiday, pupils could produce holiday guides for the year group below them, to help pupils prepare for life in the year to come. This would also be welcome across phases. Advice could come from those about to complete the first year of secondary school to those about to enter it, or advice from those having completed the first year of GCSEs or AS levels to those about to start. Giving pupils a chance to describe homework positively, will itself promote good homework attitudes. **(H18)**

◆ Some research-based homework tasks are better suited to holiday times than school times, especially when they are on rather more 'peculiar' and individual topics. 'Find the history of football' or 'Find and rank your 50 favourite designs of shoe' would be more appropriate challenges for **history** or **technology** holiday activities than 'Find the life story of Churchill' or 'Design a pizza box'.

Webquests, as mentioned in Chapter 2 on 'wandering about' homework (and explained at WebQuest.org), are good for the shorter school holidays, if on distinctive and potentially compelling topics, as pupils can get caught up in them, and cure their own boredom. **(L13)**

◆ The 'Impact' **maths** scheme has published books of mathematical holiday games (Impact project 1994), targeted at pupils aged 5 to 11 and their families. Secondary maths teachers might do well to adapt some of these games, such as spotting number plates whose numbers are divisible by 3 or by 7 (an Impact game, rapidly losing its significance as number plates have fewer numerals), which could be adapted to suit telephone numbers (divisible by prime numbers such as 13 or 29).

An interesting piece of speculation that could help take a pupil's mind off a long holiday journey would be to consider a point on the surface of a wheel. A car or train travelling at 70 mph, and not (let us hope) skidding, would mean a point on the surface of the wheel stops, accelerates to 140 mph, and stops again several times a second, with each rotation of the wheel. There must be a good homework task based on this astonishingly rapid acceleration and deceleration.

Pupils might also be asked to while away the time thinking about why they never get to the end of a rainbow, or why dogs have tails, or what makes night and day, or how much room a million Mars Bars would take up. Mathematical board games and card games can also be produced by pupils, including tasks at all levels. Indeed, as maths is one of the school subjects characterized by a love of puzzles for the sake of the puzzles, encouraging holiday engagement with maths puzzles of any kind, including puzzle magazines, can be helpful. Ideas for entertaining pupils on holiday will surely also be welcomed by parents. **(H9)**

◆ For **history**, pupils could be asked to visit a museum, having been told of local and distant museums relevant to the topics to be studied after the holiday. The homework could involve a structured report-back on the museum. Similar work could be to visit and report back on a street, house, public statue or war memorial. Having those as alternative or additional tasks would have the advantage of demonstrating to pupils that museums are not the only places to find historical artefacts.

Gallery and museum trips may be organized in school time, but if pupils can be persuaded to search out exhibitions for homework, there are opportunities for a greater variety of work, as well as a more individual experience for each pupil. A regular spot in class, where pupils report to the rest of the class on an exhibition seen, could hammock such work. Virtual trips can also be arranged in holidays or term time, as museums and galleries are increasingly available online. Having such tasks as open-ended, though still required, avoids the fear of deadlines. **(L15)**

◆ Holidays are likely to include travelling, whether close to home or to distant countries. Almost every journey crosses bridges, and holiday homework on bridges can take many forms. Tension and compression in bridges is popular with engineering and **technology** courses, and can make good holiday tasks. Sketch the bridge and then use arrows to indicate tension and compression.

The class collection of sketches should make for impressive display work, and might be given even more edge with a prize for the greatest variety of bridges seen by one pupil, or the most unusual design seen, or the most accurately 'annotated' sketch. **(L17)**

◆ The holiday suggestions can be turned around, so that for homework pupils could produce guide books for holidaymakers coming to their areas (for **English** or **geography**), or campaign leaflets to protect the beauty of the area or to highlight problems of pollution (for geography or **science**). They could plan trips to parks and rivers, including the 'artistic opportunities', for younger pupils or for their own class for **art**.

They could research detailed themes, such as bricks or leaves or gates or shop signs (for **design and technology**). What sort of people live there, and what do they do? How does it compare with other places? Are there any 'special' places in the area, places with special personal, **historical** or **religious** significance? What makes them special? Why are places the shape they are?

Most towns follow the shape and pattern of rivers, fields, hills and marshes that predated them, and have unique characteristics, ways of living and making money, accents and **languages**, religious traditions, transport networks and connections with other places. Such homework for visiting holidaymakers could be sensibly given as a set of holiday homework tasks, to which different departments could contribute, and is particularly helpful for those pupils who do not travel away during school holidays. **(L9)**

♦ Other holiday writing tasks include getting pupils to write postcards and thank you letters for presents received, getting them to write diaries and perhaps annotated photograph albums describing what they have done. When local or national issues prove important to pupils, they might be able, in their holiday time, to write a letter to a local paper, or to a local political representative, about the issue for **citizenship**.

A child with a letter published in a local paper is a child with a sense of the excitement of writing. The extent to which such activities can be captured by teachers, after the holiday, will be a measure of the extent to which teachers can hammock the holiday, in order to encourage better start-of-term activities than the popular yet often dreaded 'What I did in my holiday' task. **(L4)**

♦ There may be few opportunities in the home for putting on a Shakespeare play. Holidays filled with drama productions to which relatives and neighbours are invited seem to be the preserve of rich, fictional, Edwardian families. Yet pupils can still act, and teachers can encourage them directly or through their families.

Making videos for relatives in distant countries, or playing their part in videoed ceremonies such as weddings or family parties, can help pupils develop skills that are useful for the dramatic elements of the **English** curriculum, and can convince families of the value of homework. **(H9)**

◆ What about the pupils who go on holiday during term time? As suggested in the introduction to this section, whether the absence be regarded as 'authorized' might be determined by the pupil being willing to complete a project about the holiday, to be handed in after the holiday. This neatly changes a problematic aspect of home–school relations into one of trust between teachers and families. Here are three such homework tasks. **(H7)**

A **geography** holiday project starts with the journey. Start the project describing every detail of your journey at the start and end of your visit. Include any walking you had to do, car journeys to stations, train or plane journeys, or journeys by boat. Say how long each part of the journey lasted, how far you travelled, how fast you went, what towns you went through and any other sights you saw. You may be able to include tickets, or maps, or pictures of the boat or plane, or other interesting things you got on the journey. (You may want to do work on transport in the place you visit, too: all about the roads, buses, railways, and other ways people travel around the place.)

The place you visit comes next. Where do people live, what are the villages, towns or cities like, how many people live there, what sort of houses and other buildings are there, are there lots of visitors, are the settlements growing or shrinking, and so on? You may be able to collect postcards or other photos of the places.

Then comes work: what sorts of jobs are done? Do people work mostly in primary industries (like farming or fishing), secondary industries (making things in factories), or tertiary industries (like banks and shops, providing a service)? Are there a lot of people unemployed, or working for no money? You may be able to interview someone with an interesting job, and get them to explain what they do, and how they got into that sort of work. What do people do when they are not working, and what do they do in their leisure time?

What about the environment? What is the environment like, and how is it changing? Are there problems in the environment, like pollution or unused buildings or dangerous areas? Is the environment being improved, maybe by building new facilities, or cleaning up old ones? What do people want to improve about the place? (You could interview people, again.)

What are the physical features of the area? Mountains, rivers, valleys, seas or oceans, forests and farmland? Try to describe what makes the place different from other places, and try to get as many maps and pictures as possible, to show other people. It would be a good idea to make your own drawings, too.

The climate should be described: you could keep a record of the weather each day, and gradually build up a view of the climate of the place you are visiting. What is the temperature and rainfall? How many hours of sun are there each day? Does the climate affect what people do?

Now, compare the place you visit with your home region. Go through all the other categories, and try to work out whether they are very different or really quite similar. You could put maps or pictures of the two places side by side. You could describe what things about your home region, or about the place you visited, most surprised you. Or what you liked or hated most in each of the places. Try to explain what is *special* about each place.

A **history** holiday project could start with the people who live there. You can ask people who live there what is happening now, and how that is different to what was happening 10, 20, or maybe even 50 or 60 years ago. It is useful to ask old people, but people your own age, who have lived in that place, may know a lot about what the place is like and how it has changed.

Remember that people will sometimes disagree about what has happened, or about whether it was good or bad. Try to find out if people have really strong views on issues. People and libraries may have books about the history of the place. These can make your stay more interesting, as well as helping your history work. See if you can copy out interesting bits from books such as stories about famous events or people, or timelines of what has happened over the years. You may be able to get some pictures of famous places or events: the tourist office, if there is one, may be able to help.

Try to find out as many things as possible that pupils at your school will find exciting or interesting or useful or horrible. Buildings and other objects often tell the story of a place. Look carefully around the place you visit, and see what clues there are. You may see memorials of wars, or streets named after famous people, or buildings that used to be used by armies, or lots of other things. Ask around, and try to find out the history of the place by studying these objects.

Now, compare the place you visit to your home region and the UK. Go through all the other categories, and try to work out whether they are very different or really quite similar.

You could put pictures or timelines or stories about the two places side by side. You could describe what things about your home region, or about the place you visited, most surprised you. Or what you liked or dislike most in each of the places. Are there any historical connections between the two places? Try to explain what is *special* about each place. You might like to invent a time machine, and say what date in the past you would like to visit.

An **RE** holiday project would also start with the people. People all around the world have beliefs, and many of these beliefs can be based on religion. Try to find out about what important beliefs people have in the place you are visiting. Is religion very important? Are there several religions that people follow? Are there lots of people who do not follow any religion? Does religion affect people a lot?

Are there lots of buildings and other signs of religion, like churches, synagogues, mosques, temples or shrines? Is the everyday life of the people you are staying with affected by religion? What about ceremonies: did you go to any weddings, funerals or other religious services, or see any at a distance? Can you describe them, so that when you come back to school you can tell other people about them?

Now, compare the place you visit to your home region and the UK. Go through all the aspects of RE you study in school, and try to work out whether they are very different or really quite similar in your holiday destination and back home. You could put pictures or stories about the two places side by side. You could describe what things about your home region, or about the place you visited, most surprised you. You could try to explain what is *special* about each place.

Even without a teacher, the teacher having set this work becomes indispensable to an engaging holiday. **(L12)**

This chapter has tried to kill off homework, and has failed. Dracula-like, homework lives again, in a different guise. To abolish homework would make schooling more, not less, inequitable. Making homework homeless does not get rid of it, but merely makes the organization of the school that much more important.

Even sending homework on holiday fails to kill it off, and manages instead to help with its administration, and with pupils' enjoyment of their long weeks away from school. Having failed so comprehensively to kill off homework, it is worth admitting it has some value, and looking at how resourceful teachers can be when it comes to homework. That is the topic of the next chapter.

5 | Resourceful teachers

We need a little bit of help here, don't we?

Homework sounds as though it should be cheap, as pupils are completing school work, but outside the school and without any teachers being present. Sometimes, however, a relatively small additional investment can reap considerable rewards, and overcome a whole range of problems normally associated with homework.

This chapter looks at various ways of organizing resources for homework, additional to those described through the rest of the book. These include resources that cost money, such as setting up formal homework centres or study support facilities; they also include resources that simply need exploiting or being straightforwardly added to or complemented. There are even a few sneaky ways of developing punishments appropriate for homework.

The resources most in need of use, of course, are the pupils and teachers themselves. Therefore the final section looks at ways of finding out more about homework, in order to improve homework further. There are surprisingly few books on homework and related issues, and astonishingly few subject-based guides. Edited highlights are therefore summarized, and these summaries complement the guidance throughout the book.

1. Homework centres and study support

A reason given for avoiding homework is the inequality in resources available to pupils in different homes, especially dependent on social class and poverty. A simple alternative to abolishing homework is to provide good facilities for all pupils, the philosophy behind many homework centres and study support centres.

Back in the 1930s, there were reports of 'homework classes' that had been 'established by one Local Education Authority in certain of its poor districts'. On to the 1980s and 1990s, and Strathclyde in

Scotland decided to use its anti-poverty funding on supporting homework centres, and these paralleled support from the Prince's Trust in England for a number of after school clubs.

In the early twenty-first century, 'extended schools' (as described at www.teachernet.gov.uk/wholeschool/extendedschools/) and 'full service schools' looked to similar ways of expanding education without extending lessons. The two refrains, repeated in all of these initiatives, are that the educational impact of social inequalities should be reduced, and that the time spent *learning* is more important than the time spent *teaching*.

'Homework centres' is the phrase used, here, to cover all the initiatives including study support centres, after-school clubs, extended school facilities (where these relate to homework), and anything else that helps pupils do more studying outside classes. Such centres have been described negatively and positively. They have been described as alternatives to schools (or as compensating for the inadequacies of schools), and as alternatives to homes (or as compensating for the inadequacies of homes). Negative descriptions are likely to lead to problems, as they start with a sense of mistrust, and are unlikely to be able to build on the work of either schools or homes, merely providing a third source of learning, unconnected to the other sources.

Tempting as it may sometimes be, to give up on schools as learning organizations (at least for some of their pupils), or to give up on some homes, as sources of educational support, creating oases of learning in the middle of such deserts will be as much of a challenge as creating an oasis in the middle of a desert. It is much better to describe homework centres positively, as complementing the school's homework policy, and the support provided by homes, bridging these two sources of support.

One of the most positive versions of homework club work is the set of 'Children's Universities' that has been set up around the country. Each Children's University works across a number of schools and helps set up exciting projects for after-school work. Examples of the work of the Children's University, Hull, can be seen on YouTube (search 'Children's University Hull' at www.youtube.co.uk, with the item currently at uk.youtube.com/watch?v=Ei3A5lBdEfo).

Establishing a homework centre can be rather embarrassing for a school, if it highlights the inconsistencies in the school's approach to homework, and awkward for some parents, because the centre may be preferred to home for a couple of hours a week. Yet the awkwardness should be the source of positive developments, not defensive negativity. Schools with positively described homework centres generally improve their approach to homework. Parents if well informed are likely to get some good ideas on how to provide further support for their children.

In some ways, homework centres simply have the advantage of small classes. Pupils, when asked, frequently say homework centres are good because a teacher can be with them. As well as a teacher, small 'classes' in this way can be staffed by non-specialists, including parents who might not have the confidence to help with homework at home. They are therefore more flexible and can involve more members of the community than a simple reduction in class sizes, or hiring private tutors.

MacBeath suggested (in University of Strathclyde 1993) that teachers thought benefits of homework centres would be pupils' study habits, self-confidence, and attitudes to independent learning; the actual benefits were in practice in teacher–student relationships, achievement in subjects, and (as expected) study habits. Adults gained a better 'pupil perspective'. Teachers and pupils understood each other better, parents and pupils understood each other better. The school ethos benefited, and more equal opportunities were able to be provided.

No two schemes, of the scores currently operating, are alike. Some spend their money on staff to keep the library open before the start of the school day and at lunchtimes, some on teachers to staff '4–6' clubs for after-school work. Some arrange weekend revision courses, some set up study rooms outside the school but in community centres close to where many pupils live. What all must do is persuade teachers and other school staff, families and others in the community, and, most of all, pupils, that the homework centre is of value. Box 5.1 shows one piece of persuasion.

To set up such a homework centre, it is helpful to start with a survey of the wants and needs of teachers, pupils, parents and everyone concerned with homework. Whoever is going to be in charge of the centre should think about whether any available funds are to be used mostly on teachers, or on accommodation, or on resources. Organizers should also think of and ask about:

◆ transport: can pupils get home safely? will some pupils be unable to get to the centre?;
◆ food and entertainment or social activities: useful, but make sure they are separate from the studying;
◆ the resources that should be available: most recommend building up resources slowly, according to the wishes of centre users; and

Box 5.1

Why have a homework centre? We all want to do well, pupils, teachers, families, and others in the community. Education needs a lot of hard work. In a classroom, pupils and teachers can work with each other to develop new knowledge and skills. But education also goes on outside the classroom at home, in local libraries, and elsewhere.

We want all the pupils at this school to have the best possible chance to succeed. We want everyone to get the most out of school, to become successful, independent, enthusiastic, learners. The Homework Centre should make this easier for all of us. **(H6)**

What happens at the Centre? Independent study (which is often called 'homework') means finding out for yourself, working hard to learn new knowledge and skills. This can be a difficult business, and it may be tempting to give up at the first problem.

If you come to the Homework Centre, you will find a room with a good working atmosphere. There will not, we hope, be the distractions that sometimes stop you working the rest of the time. There will, we hope, be some useful resources, books, tables, chairs, a computer, at least one teacher (who may be able to help you with the work, and will certainly be able to provide a link with the school), and other adults and pupils who want, like you, to make independent learning easier and more successful. **(L10)**

♦ what staff can participate, e.g. teachers, library staff, older pupils, trainee teachers, volunteers from the community, social workers and counsellors, and whether they will be paid.

Once set up, how should the centre be advertised, for example, should particular pupils be targeted, perhaps in reports or on parents' evenings?

The 'cardinal principles' reported by one school were:

♦ don't think of the homework centre as extra lessons, but as helping with study skills and more independent learning;

♦ make sure there is a link to whole-school homework policy;

◆ use innovative teaching techniques (e.g. visits by authors) so the centre is seen as fashionable not 'swotty';

◆ have competitive interviews for workers, so the managers can get the workers' views out;

◆ have very senior teachers in charge, so the scheme has clout; and

◆ provide food, perhaps, but if you do, then set this up as an enterprise scheme.

'Cardinal sins', from the same people, were:

◆ do not force staff or pupils to attend;

◆ do not restrict non-academic activities, as long as academic activities can also be done;

◆ the centre must be well marketed or it will collapse;

◆ be prepared to drop staff if they do not fit the ethos of the scheme; and

◆ pupils who use the centre should get credit for being so organized.

Homework is at its best when it is more than just extended classwork, and much of this book has looked at ways of helping pupils engage with their homes and families. This should be expanded as much as possible, so that pupils also engage with, and are helped by, other facilities available in their local community and beyond. These facilities vary so much from place to place, and are accessible to different groups of people, that it is best simply to try out some approaches to developing learning in a community, beyond the classroom. The suggestions may appropriately come under the heading of 'study support', or 'getting pupils to engage with learning outside the classroom'.

There are many community groups and pressure groups, including some specialist educational groups, who aim to improve education or to use education to tackle social problems or inequalities. The groups may work outside schools, and may even set up their own schools (usually run on evenings and weekends), and this can increase their independence and distinct influence. They may also work with schools, and gain the benefits of access to the 'mainstream' and integration with well-established institutions.

Whether working outside or inside schools, community groups can invigorate, socialize and politicize; they can raise self-esteem and reduce inequalities. Pupils can be educated through such groups, although the extent to which this will help with, or be considered a part of, homework, will depend on the nature of the group and the flexibility of the school. **(L19)**

Further education colleges, adult education institutes, higher education and other post-compulsory institutions, are important sources of benefit to children's education, as adult learners not only increase their skills and knowledge, which can be passed on, but also have a greater understanding of the process of learning, which helps everyone.

The general progress of children, and the support they get with homework, must be sensitive to the provision of adult education. Supporting the homework of pupils may sensibly involve supporting the education of adults. If adults are offered genuine educational opportunities, that should be helpful. If they are only offered a narrow menu of skills-for-jobs, then the courses are unlikely to have as much impact on the education of school pupils. **(H17)**

Museums, galleries, zoos, farms, factories and fun fairs, these days, nearly all have 'education officers', and all, with or without education officers, are intensely educational. Pupils, teachers and families should make good use of them all, which means enjoying them, not treating them merely as worthy shrines to culture or industry. A good rule of thumb is to take children to museums or galleries you yourself want to visit. Then, even if the child is bored, at least you will have enjoyed yourself, and the child will have seen you enjoying yourself. That rule applies equally to teachers and parents. **(H2)**

2. Making new and exploiting old resources

Resources may be bought for homework centres, and may be available through community groups and museums, but schools will also want additional resources for 'ordinary' homework tasks. The resources most needed are good ideas; then, good ways of communicating ideas; then, material resources to support homework.

For even the busiest department or school, this can start from teachers getting together to produce a list of a small number of wonderful, supported, homework tasks for each topic or subject. If in each subject of the curriculum, there is one exceptional homework task carried out during each half term of a pupil's school career, then the overall quality of homework will most likely be considerably improved, and pupils will be more interested not only in those homework tasks, but in homework in general. Most departments when pressed come up with a dozen interesting homework tasks in an hour, so this is eminently achievable. **(H11)**

The next sources of good homework ideas are pupils. Pupils can be asked, for homework, to develop the best homework tasks for particular topics. Sometimes, this can be a competition for the present topic, with the best idea being set the following week. At other times, this can be a way of making pupils responsible for younger pupils, devising good homework tasks for the pupils about to study what they have already studied.

To stimulate such work, it can be helpful to ask pupils what their favourite homework tasks have been in the past, and perhaps their worst homework tasks, and why they have been liked or disliked. Some pupil favourites include:

- **Art**: 'Patterns, because they normally have rules, but we could really go wild, and it was explained very well and she showed us examples';

- **English**: 'Story, short but funny, and put on display';

- **Geography**: 'Draw a graph, putting information into graphs, neither too hard nor too easy, and helped in the lesson';

- **MFL**: 'Make dream school, challenging and I understood it'; and

- **History**: 'Henry VIII, it takes you back in time, enjoyable when you put your mind to it'.

Some 'worst' homework descriptions include:

- **History**: 'Filling in a sheet after a trip, not explained, just given to us';

- **Geography:** 'Gave it at end of lesson, and I didn't understand it'; and

- **Art**: 'Not good at drawing, it is not a subject where you have to read or research on it'.

There are three repeated themes from all such research. First, contrary to many teachers' expectations, pupils often prefer difficult, challenging, thought-provoking homework (if it is achievable) to easy and thoughtless homework. Second, the same homework may be one pupil's favourite and another pupil's most hated task. Third, the timing of the setting of homework and the support offered, makes a big difference to how pupils perceive the homework: setting homework at the end of the lesson is not a good idea. **(H10)**

Trainee teachers, especially those on higher education courses requiring research tasks, are relatively underused sources of good homework ideas. Their own ideas are likely to be useful and fresh and original, and trainee teachers are in a good position to work with pupils to draw out further good ideas. Using trainee teachers as 'consultants' in developing homework policy and practice, supported by higher education supervisors, gives them a status and value beyond that of 'not-quite-teacher'.

Trainees themselves are likely to have their own homework tasks, assignments and projects required of their training, and are therefore more sensitive to the issues than some other teachers. Or, rather, they might be expected to be more sensitive: a number of trainers report that trainees with problems handing in their own 'homework' are at times unsympathetic to pupils handing in homework late. Perhaps the same can be said of all in education, a profession in which everyone creates their own petards, by which they are promptly hoisted. **(H15)**

Communicating homework well can have as much of a benefit as setting good tasks. Most schools will have tried homework diaries, helping pupils remember what homework they have been set, and allowing families to check and comment on homework. Communicating homework further in advance can be achieved in various ways. One science department planned its homework tasks (as it planned its lessons) before the start of the year, and printed a booklet of numbered homework tasks. Every pupil was given that booklet at the start of the year, and, week by week, the homework was simply 'Complete task 8'.

The homework booklet could be kept at home, and adventurous pupils could try to complete tasks in advance, or catch up on tasks missed through illness, without too much trouble. Teachers enjoyed the system, as, although it took more time at the start of the year, it considerably reduced the pressure on them through the year, and pupils could ask about potential problems, well in advance. An extension of that model would involve putting that same information on the internet, now a technically very easy process. **(H4)**

If communicating homework tasks is important to pupils and their families, it is equally important to communicate with other teachers and teaching assistants in the school, and to library, computing and other resources staff. This will allow for the best coordination, the most complementary work across departments, and the most 'stealing' of good ideas.

School improvement guru David Reynolds points out that 'the range of variation by department *within* schools is probably three to four times greater than the average variation *between* schools', so that 'the typical ineffective secondary school will have some departments which have relatively good practice *when compared with all schools of all levels of effectiveness*' (in Stoll and Myers 1998). That, notwithstanding its brusque style, is the good news. The bad news is that it is 'highly likely that there will be problems within the ineffective schools in actually making purposive use of their variation by utilizing the experience and excellence of their effective departments'.

All schools, however effective, have that level of variation, and variation with respect to homework is greater than with respect to other issues in schools, so communicating homework across the school is one of the best ways of making use of good practice. This will also generate a more positive attitude amongst teachers to homework. **(H16)**

Material resources are described throughout this book, including those relatively under-used resources: people, their homes, and the communities beyond the home and school. For homework, it is best to have and develop resources that are varied, cheap and easily transportable. The variety of resources for homework should include six key formats:

◆ texts, including paper and electronic texts;

◆ pictures;

◆ music and other sounds;

◆ artefacts;

◆ moving pictures: television, DVD and other electronic moving pictures; and

◆ software, including general software such as word-processing, and subject-specialist software online or on disk.

As computing is becoming more accessible and more transportable, developing a variety of accessible resources for homework is becoming easier, if not yet easy. Each department might try to ensure that homework through a pupil's year includes at least one of each of the six formats described here.

Most already have texts and pictures, many use television, fewer use sounds, artefacts and software. The most common problems with the second set of three kinds of resource, are the lack of universal access. Not all pupils can access particular pieces of music or computers equally easily, and most departments cannot have class-sets of individual artefacts, as many are struggling to have class sets of textbooks.

One helpful strategy is to mix resources. For example, pupils might choose one of three homework tasks: either use a computer, *or* listen to a piece of music, *or* borrow an artefact. Those who choose the computer task can be assumed to have access to a computer, those borrowing artefacts can be allowed to borrow them on condition that any loss or damage would mean no more borrowing. With resources, as with homework tasks in general, working with library and computing staff in the school, and with teaching assistants, is critical to the success of the best policies. **(L10)**

3. Finding out about homework

Understanding learning and homework

To understand how homework can work, it is helpful if teachers understand why people learn (i.e. learning theory) and how people learn differently (i.e. learning styles). In recent years, writing about learning has at times been described in terms of 'miracle cures' to all educational ills, rather than in terms of academic disciplines requiring study and debate. For example, amongst the 30 or more research-based approaches to learning styles, and the dozens of research-light approaches to learning styles, some have decided that all people can be divided into those who are 'visual' (to whom pictures can be given), those who are 'auditory' (to whom we talk), and those who are 'kinaesthetic' (who use their hands). This is a distortion of its own background theory. When people say 'It works' (as is trumpeted of all miracle cures), they are probably referring, instead, to the effects of those two long-understood motivators: variety (the spice of life) and choice.

Giving pupils a varied diet of tasks will be helpful, and giving pupils some choice over what they do, will undoubtedly help. But a teacher could come to that same conclusion having read about any one of the scores of available theories. What is worth describing here is a little basic theory or, rather, two or three basic theories, that can be used in distinctive ways to help promote better homework, giving the reader some choice as to which approach appeals enough to be used and perhaps further studied.

For many decades, there have been two broad streams of learning theory, behaviourism and constructivism, with the former saying learning is driven by extrinsic rewards and punishments, and the latter saying learning is driven by intrinsic rewards and meaning-making. Whichever 'appeals', or to use an old-fashioned approach, whichever is true, both traditions can illuminate homework, and be used by teachers to develop their homework strategies.

Behaviourists tend to look at how people respond to 'stimuli' (so they may be called 'stimulus-response' theorists), which in practice generally means 'rewards and punishments'. If the theory underlying teaching is based on giving pupils incentives to do the 'right' thing, and sanctions to prevent them from doing the 'wrong' thing, then the teaching is working on behaviourist principles. The rewards may be praise or marks or stars or credits or exam results or bicycles or sweets; the sanctions may be criticism or detentions or missed breaktimes or fines. Of course, every teacher will use rewards and punishments. It becomes more 'behaviourist' if the teacher believes this is the *only* way in which to get pupils to act in a certain way.

Famous behaviourists include Pavlov (who demonstrated that dogs can be trained to salivate on the ringing of a bell if the bell has been rung every time the dog is fed), Skinner and Eysenck. Their theories are not so 'fashionable' amongst contemporary psychologists, but within schools, the practical application of behaviourist theories can dominate teachers' lives. As well as star charts and merits, a concern with physical conditions (for example, having carpeted rooms in order to reduce noise) might, if it dominates teaching, be based on these same theories.

It is an unfair stereotype of behaviourism to say that teaching is like training dogs, but it is a memorable analogy. What behaviourist approaches tend to have in common is the idea of adding extrinsic rewards or punishments, to what is happening in the learning itself, and having more rewards than punishments.

For homework, behaviourism means 'getting the buggers to do their homework' by:

◆ rewarding the completion of homework, which is all too rarely done;

◆ marking and returning homework quickly, so that the feedback 'stimulus' is associated with the original work;

◆ rewarding good quality homework, which is patchy, compared with classwork;

◆ setting up homework clubs with good conditions for studying (tables, lighting, refreshments), to compensate for poorer study conditions in homes; and

◆ being careful to avoid associating homework with punishment, and to avoid punishing pupils for failing to do something that was, in any case, largely pointless or impossible.

If pupils are to be punished for missing homework, they might best be punished by being made to complete the missing work or equivalent work, so that teachers will have demonstrated an association between the punishment and the need for learning, not punishment simply for disobedience. **(H19)**

Constructivists tend to look at each pupil's current understanding or 'worldview', and see teaching and learning as building on, or reconstructing, that worldview. Pupils are seen as active rather than passive learners: they are not 'empty vessels' into which teachers pour knowledge or 'behaving machines' that teachers can re-programme with appropriate stimuli. Vygotsky used the term 'scaffolding' to describe constructivist approaches. Helping children understand what it is that they know and can do, and giving them the tools with which to develop or change their understanding, is typical of those supporting this theory.

Classical, or more individualist, constructivists include Piaget, who sees the process of learning primarily as an individual pupil and teacher working together: pupils are sometimes like 'lone scientists'. Social constructivists include Vygotsky and Bruner, who see children as learning 'in conversation' with peers and teachers, and may look at systems (classes, families, schools, communities) rather than just at individuals.

The process of learning involves groups of pupils working collaboratively with a teacher to build up their understanding. (Vygotsky and Bruner, then, can be blamed for group work.) It is an unfair stereotype of constructivists to say that teaching is all about waiting around while pupils 'discover' everything for themselves, but it is a memorable analogy. What constructivist approaches tend to have in common is the idea of looking at the intrinsic features of learning, to support learning 'from the inside', either individually (often using 'cognitive' strategies) or collectively (using social strategies).

For homework, constructivism means 'getting the buggers to do their homework' by:

◆ 'getting the teachers to set the homework' in such a way as to allow pupils to talk about the tasks with each other and with the teacher, to ensure they are understanding how it all works;

◆ setting homework at the start, rather than the end, of the lesson, and getting pupils themselves to develop and set homework tasks;

◆ encouraging purposeful and interesting and creative homework tasks that provide intrinsic motivation or encouragement, as pupils can work long hours on tasks that really interest them, making incredible discoveries, whilst extrinsic rewards and punishments may have little effect and will never make routine and repetitive work interesting;

◆ teachers expressing an interest in the homework, and demonstrating how important it is within the subject, building relationships and conversations within and particularly beyond the school;

◆ recognizing that if pupils do not complete their homework, then they may be punished (by being given an opportunity to complete the same or equivalent work), but if pupils consistently fail to complete homework, then this may be interpreted as a learning difficulty, in the same way as difficulty with classwork may be interpreted as a learning difficulty, and referred to the specialists in special needs; and

◆ setting up homework clubs in order to bring together pupils (to help each other) and other members of the local community, to raise the profile of learning and allow more people to develop their interests out of class.

Constructivists will often say that extrinsic rewards and punishments will distract pupils from the learning: if you are working on a
project because you will get a merit mark or avoid a detention, you
will not be wanting to learn the subject, and will be unlikely to
develop a life-long interest in the subject, but will merely be learning
how to get a reward. **(L16)**

Some of the same practical conclusions can be reached from either
theoretical tradition. The 'miracle cure' conclusions, that variety and
choice help pupils work better, barely even need theories to back
them up. A strange phenomenon happens in many schools, though,
when it comes to learning theories. Teachers often act as though they
are constructivists with one group of pupils, and as though they are
behaviourists with another group of pupils. The most common
example, for homework, is to treat higher-achieving 'gifted and talented' pupils as though they are interested in the work, and therefore
need debate and discussion and scaffolding, and to treat lower-
achieving pupils as though they are only stimulated by rewards or
the fear of punishments.

An effect of this double-theory approach is to demonstrate to
pupils that higher-achieving pupils are quite different to lower-
achieving pupils, which is dangerous in itself, whichever theory might
be true. Perhaps it is based on the same principle that teachers themselves follow: on a good day, teaching is a good career because of the
intrinsic value of being an educator and helping pupils grow up; on a
bad day, teaching is a way of earning money and having holidays.

Researching, monitoring and analysing homework

Finding out about homework is valuable, and small-scale, school-
based, research can help teachers and can involve pupils in their own
learning. The research itself can be carried out within lesson times by
a teacher, trainee teacher or pupils themselves. The recent *Children's
Plan* (DCSF 2007) says that it will make the whole teaching professional a masters-level profession, with opportunities for teachers to
complete masters degrees based at work. There should be plenty of
chances to complete research on homework, to help this happen.
However, research on homework can also be carried out by trainee
teachers or pupils. One of the best pieces of research seen by this
writer was completed by an A Level sociology student, as part of her
coursework. Here are some ideas on research, and following those,
some ideas on how to monitor homework and analyse and therefore
understand the results of such monitoring.

Teachers say they set, and pupils do, a lot of homework. Research can help teachers by making them more realistic. Teachers often 'over-set' homework, in order to compensate for the fact that some pupils will do less than the teacher would like, so that the conscientious pupil will have far too much. Once a teacher knows exactly how much homework pupils do (and should do), they can match tasks to times more accurately.

The most straightforward way of completing this research is to ask pupils to write the number of minutes spent on each homework, when it is handed in, and record these minutes-per-subject systematically (for example in the homework diary), and write a spreadsheet of the results: the names of the pupils as a column, with further columns for each week of each subject, and an 'average' column. **(H1)**

One survey asked 'trios' of pupils (one achieving at a high level, one achieving at an average level, one achieving less well) how much homework they completed in each subject, for five weeks. The results were interesting in that there was little regular pattern to the results: contrary to my expectations, higher achieving pupils did not systematically do more homework than lower achievers; high profile subjects did not always have more time spent on them than lower profile subjects; a significant number of pupils completed no homework in several subjects for several weeks, despite the fact that homework had been set and completed by other pupils.

The survey surprised the staff, who realized that homework was relatively unconnected to the rest of the curriculum: some said that they had learned more about the school, through that simple, quick, survey than through any other piece of research in the school. Many concluded that the kind of homework often set, should be abolished: it was more trouble than it was worth. **(H20)**

Pupils say they get, and do, little homework, yet they find the whole business stressful. Research can help reduce pupil stress, and perhaps even increase the amount of homework done. Nearly all pupils find homework a source of stress, especially in Year 10 and above, because they *worry* about homework even when they are not *doing* homework. Ask pupils to describe the last seven days of work, having described some typical days from other research.

For example, a typical afternoon and evening may start with a return from school at around 4.30 (thinking about a rest before doing homework), having something to eat (to build up energy for homework), watching the television or playing a computer game or chatting online (and hardly ever thinking about homework), thinking about the evening meal (and not homework), eating (while family members ask whether homework has been completed), watching the television or online social networking (with homework becoming more of a worry), worrying about homework (whilst watching television), getting ready to do homework (getting the books out, but not reading them), then, at 10.00 or 11.00, doing about an hour's homework. As the homework is finished at 11.00 or midnight, the next day the pupil will go to school tired, and complain to the teacher 'I was up until midnight doing this homework'.

Research can tell the pupil that, in fact, they only did an hour's homework, and could have finished it all by 5.30 and had the rest of the evening free. It is surprising how different, how much less stressful, this feels. Indeed, if the pupil had worked through to 6.00, there would still be less stress even though there would have been an *increase* in working hours. **(H5)**

Another helpful research question concerns homework tasks. This is particularly important if the aim of the research is to make homework more interesting and effective. The simplest form of question asks pupils to describe their favourite homework task, in each subject, and say why the task was so enjoyable. Ask, too, about their least favourite homework tasks set for each subject. Such research has been used to underpin much of this book, but each department and each school will have its own patterns of favourites, depending on the approaches of the different teachers.

It may help to ask about different kinds of homework, as well as about specific tasks. Schools often say there should be variety, across oral/aural tasks, 'learning' tasks, story or reading tasks, tasks with cross-curricular significance, problem-solving tasks, and perhaps even 'finishing off' tasks. How many of each of these have been set in different subjects? **(H13)**

Alongside the time spent on homework and the tasks set, research can illuminate the best forms of support for homework. It is useful to know whether the biggest barriers to completing homework are the presence of younger brothers and sisters in the home, or the lack of books, or noise, or having too many other household chores.

It is equally useful to know whether the school could best help pupils by setting up an after-school homework club, or by telling parents more about the work done in school, or by allowing pupils to borrow textbooks or reference books.

To get answers to these questions, teachers could ask about what helps or hinders homework, or what the school could do to help with homework. On after-school clubs, teachers could ask pupils and parents about how often and for how long they would use, or would like their children to use, such clubs, if they were set up. **(H17)**

In researching and routine monitoring of homework, teachers should see if certain types of task are completed more successfully by boys or girls, and try to set a variety of tasks, and offer a variety of support, so that all pupils can thrive. Analysis of work habits, with questions about where and when homework is done (and who or what interrupts it), can be useful for the whole school to know, as well as for the pupil.

It is useful to get pupils to ask other people (such as family members or other teachers) what helps them work, or what aspects of a subject they most enjoyed, to be written up as a comparison with the pupils' own preferences. The approach a pupil has to homework may also help in the diagnosis of special needs and other problems or opportunities:

♦ Pupils may demonstrate skills in their homework that are rarely shown in classwork: they may be bullied or harassed in class, and good homework might be a sign of a block to learning in class. (It may also be a sign of cheating, or even of bullying other pupils into doing the homework for them.)

♦ Pupils may do very little homework, and on being asked about it, may admit that much of their classwork is copied.

♦ Lack of homework might indicate difficult home circumstances.

♦ A superb piece of independent research might indicate considerable untapped learning potential.

♦ The quality of a pupil's homework might be a sign of the pupil's stress level or self-esteem. As homework is a common 'stressor', when a pupil is under stress from other circumstances, homework may well 'give'. (Much the same could be said about teachers and marking/report writing, which often 'give' when the teacher is under most stress.) **(H18)**

These forms of research are complemented by published reports, from government organizations, professional bodies, and professional researchers.

What have UK government organizations said about homework?

The best known early government report on homework is that of 1936 (Great Britain Board of Education 1936). What surprises everyone who reads it, is how similar it is to those reports written half a century or more later. The interesting comparisons of primary and secondary school homework, the disparity between the amount of homework perceived by teachers and by pupils, and the variation in practice between schools, are all described then as now. It was based on surveys completed from 1935. Here is an example of home conditions:

> Except in a few cases the children return home to work in the common living room. Often a meal is in more or less continuous session, the wireless booms and the family chatters. Against such odds, work which might be completed comfortably in a short school period may linger fitfully throughout the evening.

Estimates of the time spent on homework varied from a few minutes a night to over three hours a night, with 30–40 minutes a night the commonest estimate. The report said that parents can and should be involved with homework, especially for younger children. Reference is made to the 'homework classes', as described above in the section on homework centres. These met after school in the evening, under the paid supervision of an assistant teacher, and lasted for one or two hours.

Recommending clarity of purpose in the setting of homework, along with homework timetables, homework diaries, a balance between 'written' and 'learning' homework, differentiating tasks according to pupil abilities, addressing the fact that girls complete more homework on average than boys complete, setting some longer-term 'project' homework, linking homework with classwork, and feedback from the teacher.

All of these elements from the 1930s have been present in later reports, starting with the 1980s reports (Great Britain, DES 1985, 1987). This included discussions around a survey of 243 schools.

> Those schools where homework had greater consistency, purpose and support were generally characterised by the belief that, among the teachers, an effective policy needed to involve not only the senior management team but departmental, pas-

toral and tutorial staff and be the product of extensive discussion. Moreover the communication of this policy to parents and pupils and, in some cases, the dialogue which this evoked were no less important to the policy's effectiveness than its acceptance by the whole teaching staff.

These reports also noted that 'the success of homework was related to the quality rather than the quantity of the set assignments'.

Ofsted inspected homework in the 1990s (Ofsted 1995), and gave a rather positive report, saying that most schools set homework, the quality of homework was generally 'very satisfactory' to 'good', and was seen by pupils and parents as valuable. However, there was little monitoring of homework by school managers, scant knowledge of the impact or effectiveness of homework (and it was rarely tied in to achievement), and considerable variations in the amount of homework set.

Homework got the best pupil responses when the topic was understood already, but it was sometimes set at the end of the lesson with minimal explanation or time for questions. The next government backed up the importance of homework (DfEE 1997), and provided a 'national framework for study support' and further guidelines in 1998 (DfEE 1998a, 1998b), with study support referring to 'all learning activities outside normal lessons whether they take place on school premises or elsewhere'. It is therefore a more inclusive term than homework, as it includes all voluntary activities that might help learning, as well as school-set homework. Study support therefore includes, according to these government reports:

◆ homework clubs (facilities and support to do homework);

◆ help with key skills, including literacy, numeracy and ICT;

◆ study clubs (linked to or extending curriculum subjects);

◆ sports, games and adventurous outdoor activities;

◆ creative ventures (music, drama, dance, film and the full range of arts);

◆ residential events, study weeks or weekends;

◆ space and support for coursework and exam revision;

◆ opportunities for volunteering activities in the school or community;

◆ opportunities to pursue particular interests (science, ICT, law, archaeology, languages);

◆ mentoring by adults or other pupils;

◆ learning about learning (thinking skills, accelerated learning); and

◆ community service (crime prevention initiatives, environmental clubs).

Ofsted then commissioned research on homework practice (Weston 1999), which described good practice by teachers, under the headings 'integrating homework and class work', 'tailoring homework to individual learning', 'building a partnership with parents' and 'developing independent learners'. There are also indicators of good practice on homework policies, under the headings: 'giving a lead', 'developing and disseminating policy', 'managing time', 'motivating pupils', 'providing resources' and 'reviewing performance'. The report analysed the various 'dimensions' of homework (Figure 5.1).

Over the next few years, a number of study support centres have opened, including several in association with football clubs. The government has provided more guidance for parents (DfES 2004), developed by Alwyn Morgan and Julian Stern, and more guidance for teachers (Wilson *et al.* 2004, DfES 2005), which includes case studies of good practice. Initiatives in extended schools and 'full service' schools (mentioned in the section, above, on homework centres) may help practice develop further in the future.

What professional guides are there for homework?

Professional subject guides to the setting of homework have been all too rare, although, as a result of literacy and numeracy policies, there are more primary guides to homework than in the past.

◆ A good example of a secondary subject guide for **MFL** is Buckland and Short (1993), whose suggestions can also be applied to several other subjects.

Completion Finishing off class work, 'catching up', following up what has been done in class	*versus*	**Preparation** Reading around new unit/text, research for project, learning new terms
Reinforcement Practice exercises, learning, revising	*versus*	**Research** Information retrieval, from school or home sources
Written work Essays, notes, compositions, exercises, diagrams	*versus*	**Other modes** Reading, oral inquiry, practical work, drawing, painting
Time-limited E.g. exercise timed to last 20 mins; set of 10 'spellings'	*versus*	**Open-ended** E.g. 'Research' task, TV review, practical design
Direct parent involvement E.g. parent reading with/to child	*versus*	**Pupil independence encouraged** E.g. Year 6 pupils, preparing for secondary, parental encouragement only
School resources only Homework can be completed with textbook or other school-supplied materials only	*versus*	**Non-school resources important** Pupils encouraged/expected to use library, home, family members' experience
'Overnight' task Short-term task to be completed in one homework session	*versus*	**Longer-term task** Homework used to contribute to progress of ongoing topic

Figure 5.1: Dimensions of homework, from Weston (1999)

◆ For **maths**, there is the Impact project 1994 (and Merttens 1994), for primary school pupils and their families, but adaptable for secondaries, and Weller (1996), Capewell (2003) and Pledger (2003) for secondary schools.

◆ In **science**, there are Martin and Milner (1999) and Barnett *et al.* (2000).

◆ Homework guides are sometimes indistinguishable from 'revision guides', and two publishers specialize in such guides: Scholastic (for primary, especially **English** and **maths**, see www.scholastic.co.uk/) and Letts (for both primary and secondary, see www.lettseducational.co.uk/).

◆ For **RE**, there is Stern (1998a), and RE and computers in Stern (2000) and Chapter 13 of Stern (2007).

Multi-subject guides to homework are rather rare:

◆ Stern (1997a) is one of the few paper-based guides (along with the book you are reading).

There are, however, several multi-subject websites, including:

◆ Homework High (from Channel 4, at www.channel4learning. net/apps/homeworkhigh/);

◆ the Homework Elephant (www.homeworkelephant.co.uk/); and

◆ the BBC, which has put considerable resources into homework and revision, online, with 'bitesize' revision for all ages (at www.bbc.co.uk/schools/revision/), curriculum guidance on all subjects (at www.bbc.co.uk/schools/11_16/), and guidance for parents (at www.bbc.co.uk/schools/parents/).

A good paper guide to online homework support is provided by Brookes (2003).

The best general professional guidance on homework and study support centres is that provided by Strathclyde and the Prince's Trust (University of Strathclyde 1993). There is a video and study booklets on how to promote, set up and run a study support centre, and a detailed, perceptive, evaluation by John MacBeath of various study support centres in England and Scotland.

The author of this book has provided guides for school managers (Stern 1997b), and for how schools can involve parents (Chapter 6 of Stern 2003). Other helpful general guides include Kidwell (2004) and Romain and Verdick (1997) (with the wonderful title *How to Do Homework Without Throwing Up*).

Vigorously negative views of homework can be found in:

◆ Kralovec and Buell (2000), who describe (just in the title) *The End of Homework: How Homework Disrupts Families, Overburdens Children and Limits Learning*.

◆ Kohn (2006), on the 'myth' of homework. The book is 92 per cent homework 'hates', and 8 per cent homework 'loves' (i.e. 16 pages of reasonably helpful advice).

◆ Bennett and Kalish (2006), on the case against homework. More hates, with several chapters on how to complain to schools.

It is well worth quoting an article from the *TES* (Lee 2005), that reflects the ambiguous attitude of the profession to homework. The article can be read as an attack on homework, or as an advertisement for good homework:

> When the homework policy takes effect on February 11, Year 7 pupils will carry out a research project over the half-term holiday, which will be typical of St John's determination to move away from short, repetitive tasks . . . The coverage of the homework row also brought hundreds of emails of support from as far as Australia and Japan. Dr Hazlewood said the emails reflected an almost-universal feeling of resentment about homework.
>
> 'Homework is one of the biggest sources of conflict because it is an imposition. If we can give children ownership over their learning, it sends a more positive message rather than being an additional burden.'
>
> Instead of ending homework altogether, he says the school is rebranding it. Staff expect the work to be more demanding and time-consuming. The new homework is an extension of the school's reorganized curriculum.

What research is there on homework?

John MacBeath (MacBeath and Turner 1990, MacBeath *et al.* 2001) produced what was probably the most important original, empirical, research on homework and how it is, could be, and should be approached. He noted, among many other things:

◆ Pupils should devise homework, homework should only be prescribed when it is purposeful and useful and put to use in classwork or followed by feedback, and adequate notice should be given.

◆ There is a need for inter-departmental co-ordination, discussing homework set, using seven criteria: purpose, level of difficulty, skills required, resources required, time required, range of activities, and opportunities for collaboration.

◆ Parents should be involved with homework, and should know what to do in different circumstances.

◆ Homework should never be used as a punishment, and failure to do homework should never be punished by extra homework.

◆ Initial and in-service teacher training should treat homework as an integral aspect of learning, teaching and assessment.

A range of small-scale research projects by the author of this book (Stern 1998b, 1999) looked at homework and its connection to the curriculum and ICT. Much of that material has been incorporated into the current book.

Other research from the 1990s includes an interesting study of the role of homework in the development of South African communities after apartheid (Müller 1994), an excellent set of reviews of home-school work of various kinds and in multi-cultural settings (Bastiani and Wolfendale 1996; Bastiani 1997; Wolfendale and Bastiani 2000), and a politically-significant account by Michael Barber and colleagues (Barber *et al.* 1997, and see also Barber 1996) who connect systematic homework policy and practice with success in Ofsted inspections. Barber asks how homework and performance are linked:

> It seems likely that the two are linked in a virtuous circle: the better managed a school is, the more likely it is to have a rigorous approach to homework and the more likely therefore that pupils will do more homework. That in turn leads to improved performance by the pupils and by the school as a whole.

A vital review of research evidence on homework has been produced by Hallam (2004) (and Cowan and Hallam 1999). She notes the history of reports on homework, stretching back to the 1920s, with the *TES* of 19 January 1929 having as a front page lead story 'Is homework necessary?', concluding that 'in a changing world where knowledge was available in homes and where transport meant that the world could be freely experienced at first hand, homework tasks must be of a very high educational value to justify the school extending its control into the home and encroaching on family life'.

The negative side of homework is not ignored, as homework 'can be detrimental to the individual when it . . . creates boredom, fatigue and emotional exhaustion'. On attainment, the evidence regarding the effects of homework on attainment suggests a curvilinear relationship. In other words, after a certain point doing additional homework has no more benefit. This fits well with what we know about skill development.

Pupils 'often report that homework has little relationship to the work in hand, is poorly set, marked late, and that there is a lack of pupil–teacher interaction resulting in poor feedback'. But 'despite these apparently negative attitudes towards homework, students seem to view teachers as more effective when they set daily homework'.

Homework sits alongside other extra-curricular activities as broadly beneficial: pupils 'may benefit equally from involvement in a wide range of activities not only doing homework, although it may also be that students who become involved in many extra-curricular activities are those who are already high attainers and simply seek out new challenges and activities'. Parents, according to Hallam, should not get too involved in the homework of secondary pupils.

Parents may have the most positive influence when they monitor that homework has been undertaken, offer moral support, make appropriate resources available, and discuss general issues, but only actually help with homework when they are specifically requested to do so by their offspring.

The model of homework and all the various influences on and of it, is extremely helpful for those trying to find out more about how homework works (as shown in Figure 5.2 on the following page).

And so . . .

Hallam's description of the interlocking network of factors that affect homework, homes, schools, teachers and families, is a good place to stop. Homework is here to stay, love it or hate it. Getting the buggers to do their homework means getting us buggers to set good home-work, and getting everybody to work together for what everyone wants: a well-educated next generation. May it be even better than this one.

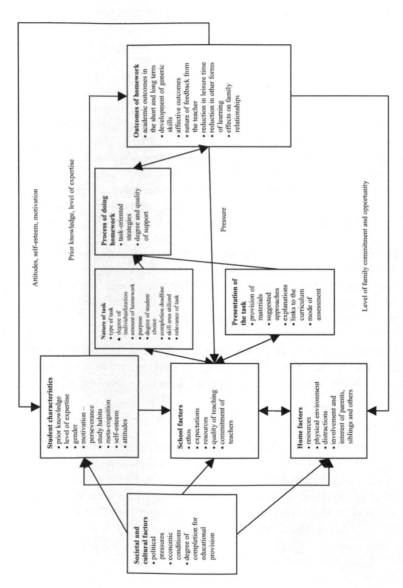

Figure 5.2: Influences on and of homework, from Hallam (2004)

Bibliography

Barber, M. (1996) *The Learning Game: Arguments for an Education Revolution* (London: Gollancz).

Barber, M., Myers, K., Denning, T., Graham, J. and Johnson, M. (1997) *School Performance and Extra Curricular Provision: A Report for the Department for Education and Employment* (London: DfEE).

Barnett, R., Brodie, M., Green, D. and Hudson, T. (2000) *Science: Key Stage 3 Homework Book* (London: Letts).

Bastiani, J. (ed.) (1997) *Home-School Work in Multicultural Settings* (London: Fulton).

Bastiani, J. and Wolfendale, S. (eds) (1996) *Home-School Work in Britain: Review, Reflection and Development* (London: Fulton).

Benjamin, W. (1999) *The Arcades Project* (Cambridge, MA: Belknap Press).

Bennett, S. and Kalish, N. (2006) *The Case Against Homework: How Homework is Hurting Our Children and What We Can Do About It* (New York: Crown).

Brookes, K. (ed.) (2003) *Top Websites for Homework* (London: Hodder Wayland).

Buckland, D. and Short, M. (1993) *Nightshift: Ideas and Strategies for Homework* (London: Centre for Information on Language Teaching & Research).

Capewell, D. (2003) *Framework Maths: Extension Homework Book Yr 7* (Oxford: Oxford University Press).

Carrington, B. and Troyna, B. (eds) (1988) *Children and Controversial Issues: Strategies for the Early and Middle Years of Schooling* (London: Falmer).

Clare, J. D. (1995) *The Twentieth Century: Options in History Programme of Study* (Walton-on-Thames: Nelson).

Cowan, R. and Hallam, S. (1999) *What Do We Know About Homework?* (London: Institute of Education).

Csikszentmihalyi, M. (2002) *Flow: The Classic Work on How to Achieve Happiness* (London: Rider).

Department for Children, Schools and Families (DCSF) (2007) *The Children's Plan: Building Brighter Futures* (Norwich: HMSO).

Department for Education and Employment (DfEE) (1997) *Excellence in Schools* (London: Stationery Office).

Department for Education and Employment (DfEE) (1998a) *Extending Opportunity: a National Framework for Study Support* (London: DfEE).

Department for Education and Employment (DfEE) (1998b) *Homework: Guidelines for Primary and Secondary Schools* (London: DfEE).

Department for Education and Skills (DfES) (2004) *Help Your Children to Learn: Getting the Best Out of Homework: For Both Primary and Secondary Parents* (London: DfES). (Also available at www.teachernet.gov.uk/_doc/7298/ 3064_HYCL_Homework_A_W.pdf)

DfES (2005) *The Standards Site: Homework*; www.standards.dfes.gov.uk/homework.

Frase, L. and Hetzel, R. (1990) *School Management by Wandering Around* (Lancaster, PA: Technomics).

Great Britain Board of Education (1936) *Homework (Educational Pamphlets, No. 110)* (London: HMSO).

Great Britain, Department of Education and Science (DES) (1985) *Homework: Note by the Department of Education and Science* (London: DES).

Great Britain, Department of Education and Science (DES) (1987) *Homework: A Report by HM Inspectors* (London: DES).

Hallam, S. (2004) *Homework: The Evidence: Bedford Way Papers* (London: Institute of Education).

Hargreaves, D. H. (1984) *Improving Secondary Schools: Report of the Committee on the Curriculum and Organisation of Secondary Schools* (London: ILEA).

Impact Project (1994) *Maths Photocopiables: Impact Maths Homework: Holiday Activities* (Leamington Spa: Scholastic).

Kidwell, V. (2004) *Classmates: Homework* (London: Continuum).

Kohn, A. (2006) *The Homework Myth: Why Our Kids Get Too Much of a Bad Thing* (Cambridge, MA: Da Capo).

Kralovec, E. and Buell, J. (2000) *The End of Homework: How Homework Disrupts Families, Overburdens Children and Limits Learning* (Boston, MA: Beacon Press).

Lawrence-Lightfoot, S. (2003) *The Essential Conversation: What Parents and Teachers Can Learn From Each Other* (New York: Ballantine).

Lee, J. (2005) 'Homework row helps pupils study: bad publicity gives Wiltshire school ideal resources for project. Joseph Lee reports', *TES*, 28 January: 10.

MacBeath, J., Myers, K., McCall, J., Smith, I., McKay, E., Sharp, C., Bhabra, S., Weindling, D. and Pocklington, K. (2001) *The Impact of Student Support: A Report of a Longitudinal Study Into the Impact of Participation in Out-of-School-Hours Learning on the Academic Attainment, Attitudes and School Attendance of Secondary School Students*: (London: DfES).

MacBeath, J. and Turner, M. (1990) *Learning out of School: Report of Research Study Carried out at Jordanhill College* (Glasgow: Jordanhill College).

Macmurray, J. (1968) *Lectures/Papers on Education* (Edinburgh: Edinburgh University Library, Special Collections Gen 2162/2).

Macmurray, J. (1991) *Persons in Relation* (London: Faber).

Martin, J. and Milner, B. (1999) *Core Science Homework* (Cambridge: Cambridge University Press).

Merttens, R. (1994) *Holiday Activities: Maths: Impact Writing* (Leamington Spa: Scholastic).

Milne, J. (2008a) 'Homework falls victim to the economic divide: more space and parental support allow affluent pupils two hour a week more study time than those in deprived areas', *TES*, 1 February: 16–17.

Milne, J. (2008b) 'Teachers call for a ban on primary homework. Conference also wants strict limits on secondary pupils' workload', *TES*, 14 March: 12.

Müller, V. (1994) *Township Youth and their Homework* (Pretoria, South Africa: HSRC).

Office for Standards in Education (Ofsted) (1995) *Homework in Primary and Secondary Schools* (London: HMSO).

Pledger, K. (2003) *Edexcel GCSE Modular Maths: Higher Stage 2 – Homework & Consolidation* (London: Heinemann).

Romain, T. and Verdick, E. (1997) *How to Do Homework Without Throwing Up* (Minneapolis, MN: Free Spirit Publishing Inc.).

Stern, L. J. (1997a) *Homework and Study Support: A Guide for Teachers and Parents* (London: David Fulton).

Stern, L. J. (1997b) 'Managing homework', *Leading Edge: The Journal of the London Leadership Centre*, 1 (3), December.

Stern, L. J. (1998a) 'Five principles of RE and homework', *Resource 20:2*, Spring, 7–10.

Stern, L. J. (1998b) *The OoSHA Review: Out of School Hours Activities in Lambeth: Report for Lambeth LEA*, Spring (Isleworth: Brunel University).

Stern, L. J. (1999) '*"It ain't so boring": Newham EAZ Homework Review: Analysis of Surveys and Monitoring*'; Report following consultancy, October.

Stern, L. J. (2000) 'Home: not alone . . . how to use computers for homework in RE', *RE Today* 17 (3), 26–7.

Stern, L. J. (2003) *Involving Parents* (London: Continuum).

Stern, L. J. (2007) *Schools and Religions: Imagining the Real* (London: Continuum).

Stoll, L. and Myers, K. (eds) (1998) *No Quick Fixes: Perspectives on Schools in Difficulty* (London: Falmer).

University of Strathclyde (Quality in Education Centre for Research and Consultancy, in association with the Strathclyde Regional Council Department of Education) (1993) *Study Support Resources Pack* (London: The Prince's Trust).

Weller (ed.) (1996) *One Hundred (Mathematics) Homeworks* (Northampton: Paxton Press).

Wenger, E. (1998) *Communities of Practice: Learning, Meaning, and Identity* (Cambridge: Cambridge University Press).

Weston, P. (1999) *Homework: Learning from Practice* (London: Stationery Office).

Wolfendale, S. and Bastiani, J. (eds) (2000) *The Contribution of Parents to School Effectiveness* (London: David Fulton).

Index